MOZART'S CLARINET CONCERTO

Mozart's Clarinet Concerto

The Clarinetist's View

DAVID ETHERIDGE

PELICAN PUBLISHING COMPANY

GRETNA 1983

Library of Congress Cataloging in Publication Data

Etheridge, David E.
  Mozart's Clarinet concerto (K.V. 622), the
clarinetist's view.

  1. Mozart, Wolfgang Amadeus, 1756–1791. Concertos,
clarinet, orchestra. K. 622, A major. I. Title.
ML410.M9E9 1982   785.6'092'4   82–20420
ISBN 0–88289–372–6

Manufactured in the United States

Published by Pelican Publishing Company
1101 Monroe Street, Gretna, Louisiana

Contents

Acknowledgments

The author wishes to acknowledge and thank the many individuals whose help has made this book possible. A special note of gratitude is due to Stanley Hasty, Robert Marcellus, Anthony Gigliotti, Harold Wright, the late Rudolf Jettel, Ulysse Delécluse, Jack Brymer, and Michele Incenzo for graciously making their time available for interview lessons and for the thorough and careful manner in which each of them imparted their knowledge of Mozart's Clarinet Concerto. Any incorrect statements that might occur concerning the respective interpretations of the concerto are absolutely unintentional and are solely the result of misunderstandings on the part of the author.

Special thanks are also given to Dorris Morris of the University of Oklahoma Press for writing assistance, Brooks Washburn and Kenneth Basdin for copying the musical examples, Pamela Weston, noted author residing in London, England, and William Scharnberg of the University of Oklahoma for proofreading, James Stoltie of the State University College of Arts and Sciences at Potsdam, New York, and Jerry Neil Smith of the University of Oklahoma for their many helpful suggestions, and to Cheryl Etheridge, my wife, for her assistance during the interview lessons at the homes and studios of the European clarinetists. Acknowledgment must also be given to the University of Oklahoma Research Foundation for the financial assistance that it granted me for travel expenses.

MOZART'S CLARINET CONCERTO

ONE

An Introduction to Mozart's Clarinet Concerto

A BRIEF HISTORICAL BACKGROUND

Mozart wrote his Concerto for Clarinet (K. 622) in Vienna during the last months of his life. He probably completed it in early October, 1791, although the exact date of composition cannot be determined accurately. Mozart's own thematic catalogue does not include the specific date that he finished the work, but an indication is given that he wrote the concerto between September 28 and November 15, 1791.[1]

Possible supporting evidence that the concerto was completed before mid-November can be found in a study by Ernst Hess.[2] Hess states that on October 16, 1791, Mozart's clarinetist friend Anton Stadler gave a benefit concert, in the program for which he possibly included Mozart's Clarinet Concerto. The most conclusive source verifying this claim, however, is a letter that Mozart wrote to his wife, Constanze, on October 7. In the letter Mozart wrote: ". . . and then I orchestrated almost the whole of Stadler's rondo."[3]

The principal themes of the first movement were drawn from an earlier sketch of the Concerto for Basset Horn in G (K. 621a), which Mozart had begun in 1789. The basset horn sketch was 194 measures long and consisted primarily of a melody and a bass line. In reworking the sketch, Mozart added bassoons and changed the key of the orchestral part from G major to A major so that the work could be played on an A clarinet.[4]

11

The concerto was dedicated to Stadler, who, according to Jean Massin, had asked Mozart to write the piece. Mozart's friendship with Stadler had previously resulted in the composition and dedication of the Clarinet Quintet (K. 581) in 1789.[5]

Documentation regarding the date of the first performance of the concerto has yet to be found. As Hess proposes, the work may have been completed in time for inclusion in Stadler's benefit concert on October 16. Mozart's statement about his work on Stadler's rondo in the letter dated October 7, 1791, may indicate that he was attempting to complete the concerto in time for a specific performance.

Of greatest consequence to musical scholars and performers was the loss of the autograph manuscript of the concerto. In a letter to Johann Anton André dated May 31, 1800, Constanze Mozart commented about the location of the concerto and quintet manuscripts.

> For information about works of this kind you should apply to the elder Stadler, the clarinettist, who used to possess the original MSS. of several, and has copies of some trios for basset horns that are still unknown. Stadler declares that while he was in Germany his portmanteau, with these pieces in it, was stolen. Others, however, assure me that the said portmanteau was pawned there for 73 ducats; but there were, I believe, instruments and other things in it as well.[6]

The first printed edition of the concerto appeared ten years after it was written. Köchel's catalogue of Mozart's works, revised by Alfred Einstein, indicates that the first edition of the concerto was published in 1801 by Andre Offenbach.[7] Johann Anton André (1775–1842), whose father Johann André (1741–99) founded the music publishing house at Offenbach, purchased a large part of the collection of manuscripts offered by Mozart's widow for purposes of publication.[8] In the same year, two slightly different other versions of the work were published by Breitkopf and Haertel of Leipzig and by Sieber of Paris.[9]

Mozart cultivated a close association with the concerto genre from early in his career as a composer. He wrote over forty concerti during his lifetime, beginning at the age of nine, in 1765, with an arrangement of three sonata movements by J. C. Bach for harpsichord and orchestra (K. 107).[10] In addition to the piano and string concerti that comprise a major part of his concerto work, Mozart wrote a number of works in the genre for wind instruments. As is the case in the clarinet concerto, all of the wind concerti were composed for specific instruments, for a definite player or client.[11] Interestingly, not one of his concerti was published during his lifetime.[12]

The concerti composed to fulfill commissions were for flute, oboe, bassoon, and flute and harp. The two flute concerti, the first in G major (K. 313) and the second in D major (K. 314), were written for the amateur Dutch flutist DeJean. The commission was arranged through Johann Wendling, the Mannheim flutist who befriended Mozart. Mozart composed the works in 1778 during his stay in Mannheim. The Concerto for Oboe (K. 271k), commissioned by the oboist Guiseppi Ferlendis, was partially completed during Mozart's stay in Vienna in 1783. Baron Thaddaeus von Durnitz commissioned the Concerto for Bassoon in B-flat Major (K. 191), a thoroughly enjoyable work that was completed in Salzburg in June, 1774. The Concerto for Flute and Harp (K. 299) was written in Paris in 1778, for the Duc de Guines.[13]

Mozart's concerti for horn and clarinet were written for two of his close friends, Ignaz Leutgeb and Anton Stadler. The horn concerti, including K. 417, 447, and 495, were composed in Vienna between 1782 and 1786 and were dedicated to the horn virtuoso Leutgeb. The autograph of K. 417 includes the following humorous inscription: "the composer . . . took pity on that ass of a Leutgeb."[14] Leutgeb, a professional horn player, was a fellow Masonic lodge member with Mozart. He also owned a cheese shop, which made him a frequent recipient of Mozart's jesting and mockery.[15]

On his return from Paris, Mozart stayed in Mannheim the latter part of 1777 and most of 1778. One of the positive results of his extended stay was his exposure to the wind players of the Mannheim Orchestra. The orchestra was famous throughout Europe for its superb blend of string and wind instruments. The woodwind section was comprised of excellent players on flute, oboe, bassoon, and a newcomer to German orchestras, the clarinet. Mozart's friendly association with such musicians as the flutist Johann Wendling, the oboist Friedrich Ramm, and Georg Wenzel Ritter, the orchestra's principal bassoonist, served to increase both his awareness of the possibilities of woodwinds and his interest in those instruments.[16]

On December 3, 1778, while still in Mannheim, Mozart included the following comment in a letter to his father: "Ah, if only we had clarinets too! You cannot imagine the glorious effect of a symphony with flutes, oboes and clarinets."[17] This comment indicates not that he had just discovered the clarinet, which he had known about from his early years, but that his interest in it had intensified after hearing it in Mannheim.

Since the Salzburg Orchestra did not employ clarinets until 1777, Mozart probably heard the instrument for the first time while visiting London as a child.[18] His first exposure to the clarinet may have been in the symphonies of Arne and C. P. E. Bach.[19] He must have been somewhat impressed with the instrument upon his introduction to it, for in 1764 he made a copy of Abel's Symphony no. 87, in which he substituted clarinets for the oboes (this copy is listed in the Köchel catalogue as Mozart's Symphony in E-flat, K. 18).[20]

According to F. Geoffrey Rendall, the first clarinetists engaged by the Mannheim Orchestra were Michael Quallenberg and Johannes Hampel. They were appointed to the orchestra in 1758 and 1759 and were later joined by Jacob Tausch. Quallenberg and Tausch were probably the clarinetists who impressed Mozart when he heard the orchestra in 1777 and 1778.[21]

Mozart made use of the clarinet in his chamber works, in most of his operas, and in four of his symphonies. His first original work that included the clarinet was the Divertimento (K. 186), composed for a patron in Milan.[22]

Only the symphonies in D major, no. 31 (K. 297), and E-flat major, no. 39 (K. 543), were originally scored for clarinets. The clarinet parts in the Symphony in D Major, written in 1775, were the first to be included in a Mozart symphony. This symphony, often called the *Paris* Symphony, was, according to Louis Biancolli, conceived in the Mannheim style. Mozart did not follow the usual practice of the day when he retained the oboe part while including clarinets; the clarinet usually replaced the oboe when Mozart employed it in his symphonies. Clarinets were added later to the scores of the symphonies in D major, no. 35 (K. 385), and G minor, no. 40 (K. 550).[23]

Mozart's smaller chamber works for clarinet include the Trio in E-flat Major (K. 498), two quintet fragments, and the Clarinet Quintet in A Major (K. 581). The Trio in E-flat (*Kegelstatt*) was completed on August 5, 1786, for Francesca von Jacquin, daughter of the famous botanist.[24] Evidence of the first publication of the *Kegelstatt* Trio, for clarinet, viola, and piano, can be found in the September 27, 1787, edition of the *Wiener Zeitung.* It appeared in this edition as part of an advertisement listing new music published by Artaria Art Dealers.[25]

The two clarinet quintet fragments preceded the Clarinet Quintet in A Major by only one or two years. In 1787, Mozart began composing the Quintet in F Major (K. Anh. 91, K. 516a). For reasons unknown the work was never completed. The second unfinished quintet, in A major (K. Anh. 88, K. 581a), was written in 1789. An interesting feature of the quintet fragment in A major is that the principal theme of the sketch anticipates, almost note for note, Ferando's aria in *Così fan tutte* (aria 24 "Ah, lo veggio . . ."). Only eighty-nine measures of the second fragment were completed. Mozart's Clarinet Quintet in A Major (K. 581) is considered by many to be one of his consummate chamber music compositions. The quintet was completed in Vienna on September 29, 1789, and dedicated, like the concerto, to Stadler.[26]

In a number of his operas, including *Don Giovanni* and *La Clemenza di Tito,* Mozart wrote prominent clarinet parts. He must have considered the clarinet part for *Don Giovanni* absolutely necessary for the success of the opera, for on September 2, 1791, he employed Stadler as clarinetist of the orchestra that accompanied an important performance of the work.[27] In two arias in *La Clemenza di Tito* the clarinet is given a role far exceeding that of an accompanying instrument. In arias 9 and 23 ("Parto, ma tu, ben mio" and "Non piu di fiore"), prominence is shared almost equally by the soprano and the clarinet and basset horn respectively.[28]

Additional information about Stadler may explain Mozart's interest in him as both a friend and musician. He was born in 1753 and died June 15, 1812, in Vienna. He became Vienna's first renowned performer on his instrument, frequently playing Mozart's works. In 1785, Gabriel Wilhelm wrote of him in Johanne Schink's *Literarische Fragment:*

> Many thanks to you, brave virtuoso! I have never heard the like of what you contrived with your instrument. Never should I have thought that a clarinet could be capable of imitating a human voice so deceptively as it was imitated by you. Verily, your instrument has so soft and so lovely a tone that nobody can resist it that has a heart, and as I have one, dear Virtuoso, let me thank you![29]

This unreserved statement of praise for Stadler appeared in Wilhelm's review of a concert held at the National Theater on March 13, 1784.

Anton's younger brother, Johann Stadler (1755–1804), was also an outstanding clarinetist. The brothers frequently appeared together in concerts; the first known concert at which they played together was for the Tonkunstler-Societat at the Royal Private Theater on March 21, 1773. In 1783 the brothers joined the eight-member Imperial Wind Band. Johann played first clarinet to his brother in this group.[30] As late as April 16, 1791, the Stadlers joined for a performance of the second version of Mozart's Symphony in G Minor (K. 550). This version of the symphony included parts for two clarinets.[31]

In 1787, Anton, who was also a distinguished basset horn player, was engaged by the Royal Imperial Court Chapel. He held that position until the final years of the century. Stadler became acquainted with the basset horn at a concert held in his Masonic lodge on December 15, 1785. Soon after the concert he learned to play the instrument; in subsequent years he earned an admirable reputation as a performer. In addition to his virtuoso ability on the instrument, Stadler improved the basset horn by adding e flat, d, and c sharp to its lower range.[32]

Though he was a highly regarded performer in his time, Stadler gained prominence in the history of music through his friendship with Mozart. About their friendship, Otto Jahn has written:

> He was an excellent clarinet-player and a Free-Mason; he was full of jokes and nonsense and [so] contrived to ingratiate himself with Mozart that the latter invited him to his house and composed many things for him.[33]

The musician and the composer probably became friends while they resided in Salzburg. Here their association was undoubtedly strengthened when Stadler was initiated into the same Masonic lodge that Mozart had joined. The two often collaborated in musical performances for the ceremonies and entertainments of their order.[34] Stadler first performed a Mozart work in 1784, when he played a program that included the Serenade for thirteen woodwinds. In his review of the concert, which appeared in the 1785 *Literarische Fragment,* Gabriel Wilhelm wrote:

> I heard music for instruments today, too, by Herr Mozart, in four movements—glorious and sublime! It consisted of thirteen instruments, viz. four horns, two oboes, two bassoons, two clarinets, two basset horns, a doublebass, and at each instrument sat a master.[35]

It is somewhat ironic that in later years this close friend sadly mis-
treated Mozart. On many occasions during Mozart's last years Stadler
borrowed large sums of money from him and never repaid them.
Upon Mozart's death Stadler was one of his principal debtors, for the
inventory and evaluation of Mozart's personal estate, dated December
19, 1791, listed Stadler as owing five hundred of the eight hundred
florins in uncollected loans and compensation.[36]

Mozart's friendship with Stadler and his esteem for Stadler's
musicianship led him to compose a number of works for the
clarinetist. Of his smaller chamber works for solo clarinet only the
Kegelstatt Trio (K. 498) was dedicated to another person. Both quintet
fragments (K. Anh. 88, K. 581a and K. Anh. 90, K. 516c) were intended
for Stadler as was the Clarinet Quintet in A Major (K. 581), the
culmination of the two earlier quintet attempts. Of the larger chamber
works it is certain that the clarinet parts of the Nocturne (K. 436), and
the Divertimento (K. 439b) were written specifically for Stadler.[37]

Several of Mozart's works for orchestra also contain clarinet parts
written for Stadler. The two added clarinet parts of the Symphony in G
Minor (K. 550) were written for the Stadler brothers, as very likely were
the parts in Symphony 39 in E-flat Major (K. 543). The clarinet parts in
two operas, *Così fan tutte* and *La Clemenza di Tito,* show evidence of
having been written for Anton Stadler's clarinet. It is certain that the
obbligatos for two of the arias in *La Clemenza di Tito* were written for
Stadler, for he accompanied Mozart to Prague in September, 1791, for
the first performances of the opera in that city.[38]

While he lived in Salzburg, Mozart completed a 194-measure
sketch of a concerto for basset horn in G major (K. 621a). This
concerto, begun in 1789, was intended for Stadler. In his initial work
on the concerto the composer notated the bass and solo parts for the
entire sketch. This is one of the rare instances in which he included
notation for the inner moving parts, although in the final measures of
the manuscript all voices are indicated.[39] The Clarinet Concerto (K.
622), presented to Anton Stadler in October, 1791, was an adaptation
of that concerto sketch for the basset horn.

By no means the first concerto composed for the instrument,
Mozart's Clarinet Concerto drew upon a rather large number of
earlier works in the genre, including works written by Johann and Carl
Stamitz, of the Mannheim school.[40] However, Mozart's concerto is of

special interest to present-day clarinetists because it is one of the best from the style period.

THE CONCERTO AND THE CLARINET

One of the salient features of the Clarinet Concerto is the use of the full range of the solo instrument. The editions published for the standard A and B-flat clarinets use the full spectrum of pitches from e to g³. There is some evidence, however, that Mozart wrote the concerto for an instrument that possessed a low range extending downward to c. Among those who have reached this conclusion are George Dazeley, an English clarinetist and scholar; Jiri Kratochvil and Milan Kostohryz, two Prague musicians; and Ernst Hess, a Mozart scholar.[41] Even without the autograph or Stadler's clarinets the evidence is still persuasive. Highly suggestive evidence may be found in later copies and published editions of the concerto, in Mozart's other works for Stadler, and in writings from the late eighteenth and early nineteenth centuries.

In the clarinet part of the present editions of the concerto a number of measures are alleged to have been raised an octave to accommodate the range of the standard A clarinet. In many other places alleged changes of octave occur in runs and arpeggios. These changes would have been unnecessary if the piece had been written for an instrument with a bottom register extending to c.

By coincidence, in 1948, both George Dazeley and Jiri Kratochvil wrote papers dealing with the clarinet part. Both reached the conclusion that the clarinet part now existing in published editions is a revised version of a concerto originally written for an instrument capable of producing e flat, d, d flat, and c. Dazeley has noted the evidence and has cited examples to illustrate this possibility, including measures 311 and 312 of the Rondo movement (see examples 1.1 and 1.2). Measures 61 and 62 of the Rondo (example 1.3) illustrate a passage in which the availability of a c (example 1.4) would make a change of arpeggio position unnecessary.[42] In most places where lower pitches may have been used, the c is sounded. This may have been in keeping with Stadler's preference for the low notes on the clarinet. (Stadler's fascination for the low register often led him to play the second clarinet part when performing with his brother Johann.)[43]

Example 1.1:   Presently accepted version of measures 311 and 312 of the Rondo.

Example 1.2:   Hypothetically reconstructed version of measures 311 and 312 of the Rondo.

Example 1.3:   Presently accepted version of measures 61 and 62 of the Rondo.

Example 1.4:   Hypothetically reconstructed version of measures 61 and 62 of the Rondo.

Kratochvil, a teacher of history and literature at the Prague Academy, and Kostohryz, a teacher of clarinet at the Prague Conservatory, directed their arguments exclusively to composition, style criticism, instrumentation, and playing technique. The result of their efforts is the probable, or possible, original versions for forty-two allegedly altered passages of the concerto. Kratochvil has developed the name "basset clarinet" to refer to Stadler's extended-range clarinet, sometimes referred to as a "bass clarinet," in order to avoid confusion with the modern bass clarinet.[44]

Several other works that Mozart wrote for Stadler provide evidence of his composition for the basset clarinet. Foremost among these pieces is the Quintet in A Major (K. 581). Both Dazeley and Kratochvil refer to passages in the quintet as additional evidence for their basset clarinet theories. Since the work is in A major, there are many places where the note c can be used on a basset clarinet in A to sound a. Kratochvil cites fifteen passages in this quintet.[45] Another probable work for the basset clarinet is the obbligato for the aria "Parto, ma tu, ben mio" in *La Clemenza di Tito,* which extends to a low pitch of c. This obbligato, written for clarinet in B-flat, is an indication that Stadler possessed both A and B-flat clarinets with lower ranges.[46] The two quintet fragments, in B-flat major (K. Anh. 91, K. 516c) and in A major (K. Anh. 88, K. 581a), were probably composed for basset clarinet as well. The quintet fragment in B-flat major was written for a clarinet capable of playing a d.[47] In 1789, Mozart drafted an eighty-nine bar portion of a quintet in A major (K. 581a). This work called for an e flat, or c concert pitch.[48]

One of the first contemporary literary references to Stadler's basset clarinet was made in E. L. Gerber's *Lexikon der Tonkünstler,* published in 1790. In an article concerned with news from Vienna in 1790, it noted that the elder Stadler (Anton) had had his instrument changed to play a third lower, thus adding e flat, d, d flat, and c.[49] This lower extension allowed the clarinet range to correspond to the basset horn, which Stadler played at the virtuoso level. The instrument that Gerber referred to was probably made by Theodore Lotz, a clarinetist, violinist, and instrument maker. Lotz had made improvements on the basset horn in 1772.[50]

In 1801, Stadler's clarinet was described in Bertuch's *Journal des Luxus und der Moden:* "Herr Stadler, great artist of many woodwinds, presented himself at a concert playing a modified clarinet."[51] The instrument was said to be bent at the lower quarter of its length, from which a wider projected opening extended, and was said to have a range and timbre in the lower register similar to the basset horn.

More conclusive proof of the existence of the basset clarinet has been offered by Ernst Hess, who quoted a review dealing with the solo clarinet part of the concerto. The review appeared in the *Allgemeine Musikzeitung* of March, 1802, shortly after the Breitkopf and Haertel edition of the concerto was published.

> Finally the reviewer finds it necessary to remark that Mozart wrote the concerto for a clarinet with an extension to a low c, so the following examples in the solo voice were displaced an octave lower [six examples

follow], and in this manner very many passages were displaced and altered.[52]

The reviewer not only took note of the changes that occurred in the later edition, but also recognized that the concerto had been written for an instrument other than the standard A clarinet. Another statement pertains to the necessity of a modified edition:

> However, until now such clarinets that extend down to c still must be reckoned among rare instruments, so one must be thankful for those additions and alterations for the normally employed clarinet.[53]

While the probability that Mozart wrote the concerto for a basset clarinet is of interest to the musicologist, it may be of even greater importance to the performer. Though the facts are not undisputed and are not totally conclusive, they add credence to a conjecture made by many clarinetists: that the technical demands presented by certain passages of the Clarinet Concerto are not in keeping with Mozart's ability to write in a highly idiomatic manner for any instrument he chose.[54] Measures 311 and 312 of the Rondo movement (example 1.1) place unnaturally heavy demands on the performer's technique in established editions. These two measures involve a rapid crossing of the register change that is repeated a number of times at a rapid tempo. This passage would have been much less difficult if it had been written an octave lower for a basset clarinet.

THE BASIC STRUCTURE OF THE CONCERTO

The melodic element of the concerto appears to be highly calculated in detail for the clarinet. In the melodic line of the work there appears to be no expressive field of the clarinet to which Mozart did not contribute in a perfect way. Viewed in its entirety, the melodic line is mostly diatonic, with skips that generally encompass smaller intervals, such as major or minor thirds. However, in Mozart's full exploitation of the differences in tone color of the various registers of the instrument, the range of the solo part frequently shifts among the low, middle, and high pitches of the clarinet. Phrases in the low register are often succeeded by groups of pitches in the upper range.[55]

Changes in register often result in extremely wide leaps in the melodic line throughout the piece. These leaps are often greater than two octaves, as in measure 90 of the Adagio movement, where the line skips from g¹ to d³. One of the intervals that Mozart utilized most frequently in wide leaps in the solo line is the twelfth. Occurrences of this interval may be observed in bars 50 and 51 of the Adagio, and bars 165 and 166 of the Rondo. Since the acoustical properties of the clarinet permit the instrument to skip from low to high registers with relative ease, extensive intervals in the solo line fit the clarinet perfectly. The least difficult upward leaps for the instrument involve the interval of the twelfth; hence Mozart must have known that the extensive leaps found in measures such as 50 and 51 of the Adagio could be performed lyrically with little difficulty for the clarinetist.

The rhythm of the concerto is for the most part regular and uncomplicated. This is not to imply, however, that it is overly repetitive or monotonous, for rhythmic clarity is one of the charming features of the work. Several extended successions of sixteenth notes occur in the Allegro and Rondo movements (one instance of this is in bars 16 to 22 of the Rondo). While the performer does not encounter rhythmic complexity in these passages, his execution of them must continually strive for rhythmic evenness.

When less regular rhythmic patterns occur, they often appear in the form of syncopations or more complex arrangements in conjunction with melodic embellishments. The most forceful syncopations are found in the Allegro, in measures 208 and 213. A syncopation also appears in conjunction with the melodic embellishment in bar 7 of the Adagio. In that measure, as well as in measures 15, 23, and 31, the *appoggiatura* on the third beat creates a subtle form of syncopation. The melodic embellishments appearing in bar 39 of the Adagio provide an example of a more complex rhythmic pattern in the work.

Additional rhythmic interest is created by fermatas followed by short indicated periods of silence in each of the three movements. When this combination of devices appears in the concerto, the rhythmic pulse is completely broken. In the Allegro, fermatas succeeded by pauses occur in measures 127 and 315. The pauses in the piece are indicated in the Breitkopf and Haertel edition by fermata signs placed above quarter-note rests in the clarinet part.

The concerto follows the style of the times in its harmony.[56] Key relationships in each of the three movements adhere to the standard late eighteenth century trend of opposing the tonic and dominant tonal centers. In the Allegro the principal centers of tonality are A major and E major. However, a somewhat progressive exception to the customary interrelation of the tonic and the dominant can be observed in the material that precedes the secondary theme of the Allegro. In this passage the solo part passes through the parallel minor key of A minor in measures 78 to 80, and also the mediant key of C major in measures 81 to 90, before introducing the secondary theme in E major. The only unusual feature of the Adagio movement is the retention of the tonic key, D major, through the first part of the middle (or B) section of its three-part formal structure. After an eight-bar delay in the middle segment of the movement, the dominant key of A major is reached. The Rondo also exploits the opposition of the tonic and dominant key centers and includes, in addition to the principal tonalities of A and E major, modulations into A minor, E minor, and F-sharp minor.

Perfect authentic cadences are utilized primarily to indicate the ends of large internal sections of each of the three movements of the work. For example, only four perfect authentic cadences are found in the first fifty-six measures of the orchestral tutti of the first movement. Deceptive cadences do not appear in large numbers, but they add to the forward motion and charm of the piece when they occur. A prime example of a well-placed deceptive cadence is that in measure 6 of the Rondo.

Tonic six-four harmony is frequently employed by the composer in climactic sections of the melodic line. In the Allegro an area of high melodic tension occurs in bars 220 to 222, and a tonic six-four sonority is maintained throughout the three measures. This classification of harmony is also utilized near the end of the Rondo in a strong melodic statement that encompasses measures 318 to 320. Another type of sonority that is often employed during climactic segments of the melodic line is the diminished seventh chord. An exemplary passage that relies heavily upon that type of sonority is the sequence in measures 147 and 148 of the Allegro movement, where diminished seventh arpeggios in the solo part carry the melodic line to a high peak.

The Allegro and Rondo movements of the concerto are more active harmonically than the Adagio movement. More specifically, the Allegro contains many diminished seventh chords and some other types of altered sonorities, such as the German sixth in measure 93 and the Neopolitan sixth in measure 216. The Rondo is the most active of the three movements regarding harmonic background. Altered sonorities in the movement include a very forceful utilization of Italian augmented sixth chords in the sequential passage that includes bars 106 to 110 and the Neopolitan sixth sonorities found in bars 81 and 222.

There is also a profusion of nonharmonic tones in each of the three movements. While the most common types of nonharmonic tones in the clarinet part are passing tones (both accented and unaccented), the *appoggiaturas* in the Allegro and Adagio movements are among the pitches that are most crucial to the melodic line. The first statement by the clarinet of the principal theme of the Allegro is one of the more conspicuous illustrations of an *appoggiatura* that provides more than simple embellishment for the melodic line. This *appoggiatura* occurs in measure 58 and in subsequent statements of the theme throughout the Allegro.

While the texture of the concerto is primarily homophonic, the work belongs essentially to the soloist, and the orchestra is for the most part limited to the role of an accompanist.[57] Interestingly, the longest tutti section in the work, at the beginning of the Allegro, lasts for fifty-six measures. Ensuing tuttis are more concise and are usually more in the nature of *ritornelli*. Since the solo and orchestral parts are extremely closely knit, there is frequent alteration in the vertical distribution of sound in the work.

The duets between the clarinet and first violins are an especially interesting feature of the work. Although brief in duration, they add warmth to the concerto and heighten a feeling of cohesiveness between the solo and orchestra. These duets appear in both the Allegro and the Rondo movements. The most outstanding example of a duet in the Allegro occurs in measures 57 and 58. Duets take place in the Rondo in bars 57 to 60, 64 to 67, and 200 to 203.

In contrast to the essentially homophonic nature of the piece, brief sections of counterpoint appear in the first and last movements. Short imitative counterpoint can be heard in measures 25 to 35 and 128 to 129 of the Allegro, as well as in measures 196 to 207 of the Rondo. An impressive example of free counterpoint occurs in bars 65 to 68 of the Allegro. In this section, the clarinet part provides a countermelody while the orchestra reiterates the first phrase of the principal theme.

Differences in the tone color of the various registers of the clarinet are exploited to a great extent in the concerto. The low, middle, and high registers of the instrument are often juxtaposed in a manner that makes their respective tone colors quite apparent. Of the many instances where contrasted registers can be observed, measures 105 to 111 of the Rondo provide an excellent example. The most obvious contrasts in registers occur when a single pitch of a higher or lower register is interjected into the melodic line, as in bars 161 and 162 of the Rondo, where in each bar an f^1 is written between pitches of the middle and high registers.

Mozart's utilization of the *chalumeau* register in the concerto is of particular interest, for he was among the first composers to discover the possibilities of the low notes on the instrument.[58] He employed the *chalumeau* register extensively in *Don Giovanni,* written in 1787, and repeated his frequent use of the device in *Così fan tutte,* composed in 1789.[59] In the Allegro of the concerto, low notes are utilized exclusively in the Alberti accompaniment figure in bars 134 to 137. Many times the low pitches on the instrument are employed in a purely melodic sense. The melodic statement that appears in measures 117 to 123 of the Allegro is written almost entirely for the low register. Bars 45 and 46 of the Adagio and bars 183 to 186 of the Rondo also were composed exclusively for the *chalumeau* register.

The tutti part of the work is orchestrated in a manner that ensures a lucid, transparent sound. The score of the concerto contains the following parts: two horns, two bassoons, first and second flute, first and second violin, viola, contrabass, and solo clarinet. The composer gave great care to the balance between the solo instrument and orchestra, in places thinning the orchestration to prevent the overpowering of the clarinet.[60] For example, passages occur in the Adagio where the contrabass remains silent, such as in the opening statement of the principal theme in bars 1 to 8 (this also occurs in bars 17 to 24, 72 to 75, and 92 to 94).

In the broadest description of its form, the concerto contains three movements that are given the tempo indications Allegro, Adagio, and Allegro. The length in measures of each of the three movements respectively is 359, 98, and 353.

The structure of the initial Allegro (example 1.5) closely parallels the first movements of a number of Mozart's other concerti, with an opening tutti and subsequent exposition, development, and recapitulation sections. In addition to the initial tutti, orchestral *ritornelli* occur after the exposition and the development and in the coda of the movement. As can be observed in a number of Mozart's other concerti, the secondary theme is omitted from the opening tutti of the Clarinet Concerto, appearing in the solo exposition.[61] Thematic material of the movement is expanded such that each principal subject includes a group of two or more themes.

Example 1.5:   Form of the initial Allego movement.

1–56	57–153	154–71	172–227	228–48	249–315	316–43	344–59
Tutti	Exposition	Tutti	Development	Tutti	Recapitulation	Closing Section	Tutti

The Adagio (example 1.6) is in three-part form. The first section reappears in abbreviated form after the cadenza. The cadenza follows the second (or B) section of the movement.

Example 1.6:   Form of the Adagio movement.

1–32	33–58	59	60–93	94–98
A Section	B Section	Cadenza	A Section	Coda

The final movement of the concerto is in sonata rondo form, which is essentially a five-part rondo with coda (example 1.7). The C section functions as a developmental section. At measure 334 in the coda there is a brief reference to the rondo theme.

Example 1.7:   Form of the final Allegro or Rondo movement.

1–56	57–113	114–37	138–246	247–300	301–53
A	B	A	C	A	Coda

Periodic structure in the three movements is regular and for the most part evenly balanced. Antecedent and consequent phrases average four measures in length. Phrases of irregular length do occur, as in measures 65 to 75 of the Allegro. In this section a four-measure antecedent phrase is followed by a seven-measure consequent phrase. In a number of sections the dividing line between periods is obscured. The most common method utilized for division is the placement of a half cadence in a strong position at the end of a phrase group, thus giving the penultimate sonority a sense of finality. In bar 36 of the Allegro, for example, the closing chord sounds final. However, the sonority is based on the subdominant. Endings of formal sections and phrases are also obscured by elision. An outstanding example of this is found in measure 100 of the Allegro, where a dominant sonority provides both a final chord for the principal theme group and a beginning for the secondary theme group.

TWO

Stanley Hasty's Interpretation

Stanley Hasty's musical background includes study with several prominent clarinet teachers and positions in a number of the leading symphony orchestras of the United States. He cites Rufus Arey, a former teacher of clarinet at the Eastman School of Music of the University of Rochester, and Ralph McLane, a former clarinetist with the Philadelphia Orchestra, as the two teachers who have most influenced his playing. During his career as a professional clarinetist Hasty has held positions with the Pittsburgh, Cleveland, and Rochester symphony orchestras. While solo clarinetist of the Pittsburg Symphony, he performed the Mozart Clarinet Concerto under the baton of William Steinberg; in Rochester he played the work with Lazlo Smogi as conductor. Hasty is presently professor of clarinet at the Eastman School of Music. He considers his rendition of Mozart's Clarinet Concerto to be the product of his musical training, his professional experience, and his own musical thinking as it has developed over a number of years.

In his interpretation of the concerto, Hasty attaches particular importance to three elements of the work: the melodic line, the harmony, and the formal structure. Each of these elements, which he regards as determining factors in interpretation, is considered in his choice of dynamic levels, articulations, and development of devices related to musical expression, such as *tenuto* effects, dynamic phrasing, and dolce and grazioso playing.

Features of the melodic line to which Hasty gives the greatest emphasis are interval relationships within the individual phrases, changes of direction in the line, and repeated pitches. Within the context of the harmonic structure of the concerto, the actual harmonic progression, including chord changes and the resolution of dissonance, plays a prime role in his interpretive judgments. Altered chords, nonharmonic tones, and modulations are also given consideration in the area of harmony. The formal structure of the concerto, including both the overall form of the three movements and the periodic and singular phrase structure of individual movements and sections, is carefully recognized and is frequently the basis for interpretive decisions.

According to Hasty's interpretation, dynamic phrasing is determined both by the melodic line and by its underlying harmonic structure. The first factor is the contour of the melodic line; diatonic movement and leaps very often call for changes in dynamics. A change of the chord member in the melodic line is the second factor that must be taken into account. This concept, as well as that of dynamic change in conjunction with tension and release of tension, is primarily dependent upon the harmonic underpinning of the melodic line.

It is Hasty's opinion that articulation is useful primarily for emphasis. This is especially true of his approach to articulation in the concerto. Other functions of articulation are to separate pitches and to maintain symmetry within the melodic line. Articulation can be used to stress changes of direction and conjunct movement within the line. In a similar sense, it may be employed to accentuate changes in harmony and nonharmonic tones and to make altered chords more apparent to the listener. In runs comprised of uneven numbers of pitches, articulation can be utilized to add emphasis within the run to create a sense of evenness and completion.

ALLEGRO MOVEMENT

In his approach to the melodic line of the opening Allegro movement, Hasty concentrates on the emphasis of specific nonharmonic tones in the principal theme and the succession of intervals found in the beginning of the secondary theme group. The *appoggiatura* figure of the principal theme, found in measures 57 and 58 (example 2.1) and in subsequent statements in the remainder of the movement, receives special attention. It serves as a basis for the determination of emphasis of both pitches and dynamic phrasing in phrases of similar construction and for the treatment of other non-harmonic tones. The successions of major or minor thirds near the beginning of the subordinate theme group frequently appear within developmental material in the movement. Consequently, they are somewhat isolated by the added expression that they receive.

Example 2.1

Measure 58 of the opening statement in the solo part begins with an a³. This pitch is a nonharmonic tone that is approached by leap from an f³ in the preceding bar. It resolves downward to a g³ on the second half of the first beat of bar 58 in a manner similar to an *appoggiatura.* Hasty believes that in this statement the ascending major third interval should be played espressivo. In order to permit this, the upper note of the interval must not be tongued. The descending notes that follow the a³ in measure 58 are intervals of major and minor seconds, which must also be performed espressivo. Similar examples of this can be found in measures 84 and 85, 116 and 117, 120 and 121, and 129 and 130.

Other situations which are influenced by his approach to measures 57 and 58 include measures 103 and 104 and the trill in bar 74. Measures 103 and 104 (example 2.2) involve a minor third interval from f³ sharp to a³ (measures 117 to 120, 172 and 173, and 176 and 177 possess similar melodic structures). This interval is also played expressively. The trill in measure 74 is executed from the note above, in keeping with the pattern established by the *appoggiatura* figure in measures 57 and 58.

Example 2.2

The succession of intervals found at the beginning of the secondary theme group provides an equally important archetype for subsequent melodic interpretation. This melodic figure, which first appears in measure 79 (example 2.3) is comprised of three successive major or minor thirds. Whenever this succession of intervals appears, the pitches are played by Hasty in an espressivo manner. The notes are slightly lengthened, building to a crescendo at the top pitch. Very often, as in measure 79, the highest of the three included pitches is the seventh of the chord. When the outlined triad is repeated, as in measures 79 to 83, it is played more insistently with each reiteration.

Example 2.3

Applications of the espressivo succession of thirds can be found in measures 87, 89, 90, 106, 116, and 120. As shown in example 2.4, the series of triads outlined in measures 87, 89, and 90 grow increasingly more forceful and insistent. The triad in bar 89 is played slightly more marcato than the triad in 87, and the series of pitches in measure 90 is the most marcato of the three. In measure 106 the triadic structure of the line is emphasized by a crescendo and a slight increase in length on the three pitches. Again, in measures 116 and 120 (example 2.5), the triads, which are both comprised of identical pitches, should be played molto espressivo. (The top pitches of the melodic line in bars 116 and 120 provide the seventh to the dominant harmony sounding in the tutti.) The melodic structure of measures 174, 178, 308, and 309 also includes a succession of major and minor thirds; therefore, they are treated in a similar fashion.

Dynamic level alterations are often controlled by changes of position of the soprano line in relation to the harmonic background. According to Hasty, changes in the position of the melodic structure relate to intervallic leaps in the solo line within the context of the same chord. A prime example of this concept can be seen in bars 108 and 109 (example 2.6). In these two measures the pitches on the fourth

beats are members of the same chordal structure as the groups of
notes on the third beats. In addition to a higher dynamic level on each
of the succeeding groups, the tension that is built on the first group of
each measure is relaxed on the fourth beat.

Example 2.4

Example 2.5

Example 2.6

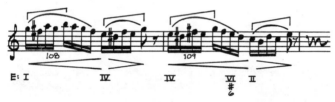

When a change of position in the soprano line does not occur,
dynamic fluctuation is usually determined by the contour of the
melodic line. In bar 110 (example 2.7) a change of harmony is felt on
each of the four beats. Unlike the two preceding measures, a change of
position does not take place in the melodic line in bar 110; the
dynamic level consequently increases with the ascending pitches and
diminishes when the line descends.

Example 2.7

Dynamic phrasing is also utilized to accentuate altered harmonies
in the Allegro movement. As can be seen in example 2.8, the b^2 flat in

measure 216 begins forte and gradually diminishes to the c^1 sharp in bar 217. This is done to call attention to the Neopolitan sixth in 216 and the secondary dominant harmony in 217. The a^3 in 218 begins piano and crescendoes to the d^1 sharp in 218. Tension built in 218 is released through a diminuendo in 219. The dynamic phrasing in measures 218 to 220 highlights the diminished seventh chord in 219.

Example 2.8

Hasty's choice of dynamic levels in the Allegro is often influenced by the internal phrase structure. Repeated phrases and sequential material are nearly always assigned different levels of volume. The line in bars 182 to 184, which recurs immediately in 184 to 186, is introduced at the forte level and played piano on its repetition (example 2.9).

Example 2.9

Sequential passages occur in measures 145 to 147, 150 and 151, 184 to 186, and 220 to 223 of the developmental section of the Allegro. The sequence in bars 220 to 223, for example, begins piano, and each successive section of the sequence is played at a higher dynamic level (example 2.10).

Example 2.10

In measures 206 to 209 and 280 to 282, Hasty carries the phrase groups across the bar lines. The phrases in 206 to 209 begin on the second beat of the initial measure and end on the first beat of the succeeding measure. These four-beat groupings are begun by tonguing and are slurred to their endings. As is indicated in example 2.11, the phrases in measures 280 to 282 are divided on the first half of bar 281.

Example 2.11

While the internal phrase structure of the Allegro plays a prominent role in interpretive decisions, the larger sections of the formal structure are considered as well. Large sectional units are generally treated in the same manner each time they appear. Dynamics, phrasing, and articulations are not changed on the return of either the principal or the secondary theme groups. This approach is also followed for the closing sections of the exposition and recapitulation. Both of these sections, beginning respectively in measures 128 and 316, are treated as concluding material. According to Hasty, the consistency of style is beneficial to the listener. "One of the charms of the piece is the return of an idea; the listener recognizes it."

The end of the transition between the principal and secondary theme groups that takes place in measure 100 is interpreted as both a formal and a harmonic device. In terms of the form, measure 100 represents an elision. The sustained d^2 in the solo part provides both an ending for prior transitional material and a beginning of the secondary theme group. Harmonically, the d^2 is a member of a chord that is a part of the modulation from B to E major. The b^2 (concert) in the clarinet part becomes the root of the dominant in the the new key.

Hasty feels that the d^2 in the clarinet part provides a stronger feeling of transition if it is held longer than its written duration. This quasi cadenza (example 2.12) can be played with little danger of ensemble problems because the tutti part has rests on the second through fourth beats of the measure. In keeping with the concept of similar treatment of large formal sections, the g³ (concert) in measure 288 is also played as a quasi cadenza.

Example 2.12

Another quasi cadenza appears in measures 198 and 199. Preparation for this passage is made in bar 197, through a crescendo and ritardando on the last three quarter notes. The harmonies in both measures 198 and 199 are held while the solo part is played as a sort of quasi cadenza, in *rubato* fashion (example 2.13). The solo part returns to the original tempo near the end of measure 199.

Example 2.13

The fermatas in measures 127 and 315 of the Breitkopf and Haertel edition are retained in Hasty's interpretation. In measure 127 (example 2.14) the first fermata is given the time of three quarter notes in the established tempo, and the held note on the third beat is allowed the time of two quarter notes in the original tempo. Since bar 315 is part of a repeated section of the movement, it is treated in the same manner.

Example 2.14

Articulations in the Allegro movement are chosen in accordance with Hasty's principles of emphasis, separation of pitches, and melodic symmetry. In addition to these points, articulation is called upon for espressivo and grazioso passages, and sometimes merely for the sake of variety.

In measure 103 (example 2.2), the return of tonic harmony is accentuated by tonguing the b^2 on the first beat. An important instance of separation of pitches is found in bar 94, where each of the three notes is stopped by the tongue. The tongue provides the release for the beginning of the second and third eighth notes, in order to create a separated but melodic effect.

Hasty's use of articulation in espressivo and grazioso passages is of the greatest importance in his interpretation of the concerto. Gradations of articulation from molto legato to marcato are utilized in the Allegro. Molto legato tonguing is used in measure 71 (example 2.15), bar 87 (example 2.4), and on the third and fourth eighth notes of bar 130. As previously noted, measure 90 (example 2.4) is articulated in a marcato fashion. Grazioso effects are introduced in both new and repeated material. Measure 73 (example 2.16) is not reiterated material; however, the sixteenth notes in the second half of the measure are tongued. Detached notes on a repeated phrase for a grazioso effect are found in measure 182 (example 2.9).

Example 2.15

Example 2.16

Articulations are utilized for the sake of variety in two sequential passages occurring in bars 145 to 147 (example 2.17) and 334 to 336, which are identical in pattern. As each of these sections progresses, fewer notes in the sequences are tongued.

Example 2.17

It should be noted that more articulations are removed by Hasty from the Breitkopf and Haertel edition than are added. This is especially true in long series of sixteenth notes in which changes of direction do not occur or in which Hasty desires longer phrase groupings. Among the places that articulations are deleted from are measure 73 (example 2.16), bars 83 and 84 (example 2.18), measures 148 and 149 (example 2.19), and in measures 182 and 184 (example 2.9).

Example 2.18

Example 2.19

Changes of notation in the Allegro are made in measures 146 to 148 and 333. The second and third beats of measures 146 and 147 (example 2.17) are transposed upward one octave. These octave shifts provide for greater expansion of the arpeggios, and may be in keeping with the alleged original edition for the basset clarinet. The first two beats of measure 333 are also transposed an octave higher. The addition of the low g^1 on the second sixteenth note of measure 148 (example 2.19) is somewhat unusual. Hasty believes that the added note gives the passage greater impetus and a more thorough sense of completion.

ADAGIO MOVEMENT

In Hasty's basic interpretation of the Adagio, the melodic line is played in a dolce, espressivo manner. As in the Allegro, the intervallic relationships of the principal theme are given special emphasis. In measure 1 of the first phrase (example 2.20) the solo line contains leaps of a perfect fourth and a major third. These upward skips are played very expressively and intensely. The tenseness relates to a sense of direction and anticipation of the release of tension. The descending major seconds of the second measure are played dolce. These pitches release the tension that is built in the first measure.

Example 2.20

Measures 5 and 6 (example 2.21) are interpreted in a reverse fashion. The eighth notes in bar 6 are played in an espressivo manner (this is one of the few instances in the concerto where descending intervals are played expressively). The two eighth notes in measure 22, which recur in bar 73, are also played espressivo, as are the two sixteenth notes on the first half of the third beat of measure 93.

Example 2.21

According to Hasty, the grace note in measure 7 of the solo part (example 2.22) must be executed without detracting from the time value of the quarter note that precedes it. Example 2.22 provides a close approximation of the rhythm in which the grace note and pitches of the third beats of measures 7, 23, 66, and 82 are played. It is Hasty's opinion that the grace notes must be played on the third beat and be given a slightly shorter duration than that of the sixteenth note on the last quarter of the third beat.

Example 2.22   Written:

Played:

Unlike the trills in the Allegro, the two trills in the Adagio are not played as inverted trills. The trills, found in measures 53 and 92, are both initiated from the written pitch. The basis for this interpretive decision lies in Hasty's preference in these two instances for the sound of noninverted trills, not in stylistic considerations.

When not made in conjunction with espressivo gestures, dynamic changes in the second movement are closely related to the formal structure. In terms of the overall form, Hasty gives strong recognition to the middle and return sections of the three-part form. In his interpretation the middle section, including measures 33 to 59, is dealt with as a single phrase. This segment of the Adagio is played at a louder dynamic level than the first section and becomes increasingly more rhapsodic as it progresses toward the cadenza. In contrast to the outwardly focused B section, the return of the A section after the cadenza affords a complete change in mood and volume level. Measures 60 to 67 are played *sotto voce,* which is in opposition to the established pattern of identical dynamic levels for repeated sections of the formal structure. In compliance with the pattern begun in the Allegro, measures 69 to 82 are performed at the same dynamic level as bars 19 to 24.

The internal phrase structure also weighs heavily in the determination of dynamics. The second phrase of the solo part, bars 17 to 24 (example 2.23), is played louder than the opening statement, but in the same dolce-espressivo context. The sequential development of the second phrase is also reflected in higher dynamic levels in each of the three segments.

Example 2.23

Treatment of immediate repetition in the melodic line follows the precedent set in the Allegro. Since the solo and tutti parts are identical in measures 84 and 85, bar 85 is played at the pianissimo level to create an echo effect. Because the solo and tutti parts of bar 88 are different from bar 89, Hasty does not reiterate the latter measure at a quieter dynamic level, as many performers do. In place of the echo effect between the two measures, Hasty crescendoes from the end of measure 88 through the beginning of bar 89 (example 2.24).

Both the first and the second phrases of the closing section are begun at higher dynamic levels than indicated in the Breitkopf and Haertel edition. These phrases, which begin in measures 83 and 87, are initiated at the mezzo piano and mezzo forte levels respectively.

One of the most striking features of Hasty's interpretation of the Adagio is his addition of a brief pause after the g^1 on the first beat of bar 90, and the entrance of the succeeding d^3 and c^3 at the *sotto voce* level (example 2.24). A slight ritard is made on the third beat of measure 89 and the first eighth note of bar 90. The dynamic level preceding the pause is mezzo forte, and the performer returns to a higher level of volume after the *sotto voce* d^3 and c^3. The pause and ensuing entry at *sotto voce* serve to accentuate the wide leap from g^1 to d^3. In terms of the harmonic background, the halt in bar 90 is made after a plagal cadence.

Example 2.24

Other changes in rhythm occur in measures 93, 95, 96, and 98. The deceptive cadence on the first beat of measure 93 (example 2.25)

again halts the motion. Before the tempo is resumed on the sixteenth-note triplets in the second half of the third beat, the duple sixteenth notes on the beat are played espressivo. The first and third beats of bar 95 (example 2.26) are extended, and the original tempo is resumed by the orchestra on the second beat of measure 96. In the final measure, the tutti part stops on the second beat, and the solo part may be held longer than the half note that is written.

Example 2.25

Example 2.26

The cadenza should be short and original. As a guideline for the content of the cadenza, Hasty believes that the performer should quote Mozart rather than himself. Example 2.27 represents the cadenza developed by Hasty, which duplicates the written cadenza of Mozart's Clarinet Quintet with the addition of a dominant-seventh arpeggio beginning on b^2 flat and extending downward to low e^1. The cadenza begins with a strong dynamic level and ends *sotto voce*.

Example 2.27

Changes made by Hasty in the notation and articulations of the Breitkopf and Haertel edition are minimal in the Adagio. The only change of notation occurs in bar 73, where a b^3 flat is added on the second half of the first beat so that the notation conforms with measure 22. Articulation changes consist of the addition of slurs to create a greater sense of continuity within phrases or to carry phrases across bar lines to their final notes. To preserve continuity, slurs are added in measures 5 and 6 (example 2.21), in bar 33 (example 2.28), and between measures 90 and 91 (example 2.24). In measures 95 and 96 (example 2.26), slurs are added to carry the two phrase groups across the bar lines to their final notes.

Example 2.28

RONDO MOVEMENT

A major part of Hasty's interpretation of the Rondo may be understood with regard to his usage of articulation in the movement. This is not to say, however, that he uses the Rondo as a vehicle for the display of rapid tonguing. Articulation plays an important role in interpretation of the melodic line, emphasis of the harmonic background, phrasing, effects, and the preservation of symmetry in a number of runs in the movement. In his approach to the melodic line, Hasty uses the tongue for additional emphasis of pitches, expressive playing, separation of notes, and connection of pitches in awkward skips. Among the instances in the Rondo where the emphasis of the melodic line is sharply defined in his interpretation are measures 1, 6, 63, 67, and 311 to 313.

Hasty believes that the basic framework of bars 1 and 2 (example 2.29) is comprised by the g^2 and a^2 on the first and fourth beats of measure 1, and the f^2 and e^2 on the first and fourth beats of the second bar. The remaining sixteenth notes after the fourth beat of measure 1 act as embellishment to the line. In order to accentuate the main melodic substance of the two measures, the triple g^2 and the a^2 and f^2 are tongued.

Example 2.29

The beginning of the succession of sixteenth notes in measures 6 and 7 is emphasized by articulating the c² on the sixth beat of measure 6. The line itself is again stressed in measure 63 (example 2.30) by legato tonguing on the second through the sixth eighth notes. Tonguing is again utilized in measure 67 (example 2.31) to accentuate the third and sixth eighth notes. In this case the emphasized pitches represent changes of direction in the melodic line. The predominant pitches in the series of sixteenth notes in bars 311 to 313 are also made more distinct through articulation (example 2.32). It is Hasty's belief that the melody in the lower notes of the passage may in fact be stressed by tonguing or slurring any of the pitches involved.

Example 2.30

Example 2.31

Example 2.32

Legato tonguing is employed on the final two eighth notes in bar 4, and on subsequent recurrences of the principal theme of the Rondo. Hasty's interpretation of these two eighth notes (example 2.33) is the first appearance of espressivo playing in the movement.

Example 2.33

As indicated in the Breitkopf and Haertel edition, the c^2 and b^2 flat of bar 202 (example 2.34) are tongued. This articulation is deemed necessary for separation of the melodic line at this point. Another passage in which separation of the line is desirable is the one beginning in bar 301. The sixteenth notes in measures 301 to 305 (example 2.35) should be tongued, if possible, to create a feeling of separation and hesitation. According to Hasty, this effect can also be achieved if the performer slurs the second half of each of these measures.

Example 2.34

Example 2.35

The awkward downward skip from the d^3 in bar 176 to the c^2 on the first beat of bar 177 (example 2.36) is made easier by tonguing the c^2 in bar 177. Articulation not only overcomes the inherent difficulty of making changes from higher to lower partials of the overtone series, but also results in a better connection of the two pitches.

Example 2.36

As in the preceding movements, articulations of the Breitkopf and Haertel edition are removed from the Rondo to create a greater feeling of continuity in the melodic line. Specific measures where tonguing is eliminated include bars 20 and 21, 36, 69 and 70, 84 and 85, 88 and 89, and 174 to 176. All but the first notes of measures 20 and 21 are slurred in Hasty's rendition (example 2.37). The c^3 in measure 36 is not tongued because Hasty believes that it is not of greater importance than the surrounding pitches. As in bars 20 and 21, a greater feeling of expansiveness and connection is achieved through the addition of slurs in measures 69 and 70 (example 2.38). The slurred groups of sixteenth notes included in the first and fourth beats of bar 69 and in the first beat of bar 70 are extended to include the following two beats of each of the groups. Similar extensions of shorter slurred groups are made in bars 84 and 85 (example 2.39) and bars 88 and 89 (example 2.40). In measures 174 to 176 (example 2.41) short groups of notes and complete measures are connected by a single slur.

Example 2.37

Example 2.38

Example 2.39

Example 2.40

Example 2.41

In a number of passages in the final movement, articulation is drawn upon to highlight chord progressions and altered sonorities in the harmonic background. While a standardized formula for the determination of articulations does not exist in any of the three movements, strong chordal progressions, unusual or unanticipated cadences, and some of the less frequently used altered chords are often considered in Hasty's decisions about tonguing.

The half cadence on the dominant in measure 4 provides an example of a somewhat delayed harmonic progression together with the emphasis of a cadence. Hasty slurs from the preceding bar to the c^2 on the first beat of bar 4, a note that is a member of the subdominant chord. He then tongues the second through the fourth beats so that the main emphasis of the line will fall on the d^2 that is part of the dominant harmony.

Articulation is utilized in measure 7 to accentuate a change of harmony from the subdominant on the first three beats to the dominant on the second half of the measure (example 2.42). Each of the sixteenth notes at the beginning of the bar is tongued. The two sixteenth notes on the fourth beat are slurred, thus giving more emphasis to the b^2 on that beat. This calls the listener's attention to the change of harmony that occurs in the second half of the measure.

Example 2.42

A similar pattern of articulation is employed in bar 22 (example 2.43). Since the entire measure represents a change of harmony from bar 21, however, the two sixteenth notes on the first and fourth beats are slurred. In measure 22 the g^1 and g^2 become the most prominent pitches.

Example 2.43

Nonharmonic tones in measures 37, 93, and 111 are also given additional emphasis through articulation. The c² sharp of the first beat of bar 37 is tongued and given more dynamic weight than surrounding pitches. For an increase in emphasis the f² sharp pitches in measures 93 (example 2.44) and 111 (example 2.45) are also tongued. The accentuation of these nonharmonic tones focuses even greater attention on the altered harmonic backgrounds of the two measures.

Example 2.44

Example 2.45

Hasty illuminates the altered chords in bars 94 and 104 by articulating notes of the accompaniment chords that appear in the solo part. The pitches that are tongued are the c² sharp in measure 94 (example 2.44) and the f² sharp in bar 104 (example 2.46). Both of these accentuated altered sonorities are German sixth chords.

Example 2.46

The internal formal structure of the Rondo affects Hasty's use of both articulation and dynamics. Since Hasty's conception of the phrase structure in measure 3 (example 2.47) is closely aligned with articulation, the two eighth notes at the beginning of that measure are not given as short a duration as the eighth note on the fourth beat. It is Hasty's belief that the first two eighth notes are inside the phrase and therefore must maintain continuity, whereas the fourth beat eighth note ends the phrase.

Example 2.47

Effects in the Rondo to which articulation lends itself include changes of character within phrases and grazioso performance of reiterated material. With the e^2 on the third beat of measure 82, there is a change from legato dolce to scherzando in nature, moving toward the completion of the cadence in bar 84 (example 2.48). The e^2 in bar 82 is tongued to separate it from the preceding legato dolce material. As in the Allegro, the second of two identical short phrases closely following one another is frequently played grazioso. The reiteration of the arpeggio in bar 84, which occurs in bar 86, is tongued instead of slurred for a grazioso effect (example 2.49). Measure 61 (example 2.50) provides another instance of a passage that is performed grazioso.

Example 2.48

Example 2.49

Example 2.50

In order to maintain the symmetry of odd-numbered groups of sixteenth notes, such as the groups occurring in measures 43, 47, and 159, slurs can be introduced on even-numbered beats within the runs. The addition of slurs between the two sixteenth notes of the second and fourth beats of bars 43 and 47 (example 2.51) serves to reestablish a sense of evenness and completeness in the passages. In a similar manner, the introduction of slurs between the two sixteenth notes on the second and fourth beats of measure 160 (example 2.52) adds a greater sense of balance and symmetry to this group of pitches.

Example 2.51

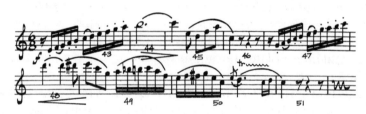

Example 2.52

Dynamics are utilized in the Rondo movement to enhance the expressiveness of the music, to create effects, and to maintain balance between the solo and orchestral parts. Hasty's general principles of dynamic phrasing—that is, determination by melodic line and under-lying harmonic structure—remain in effect in the Rondo. However, several passages provide clarification or deviate in some way from his basic concepts. When not in conjunction with individual espressivo notes, dynamic changes are made to clarify the phrase structure, including the larger formal elements, and to emphasize tension and release of tension in the melodic line. In the phrase structure of bars 43 to 51 (example 2.51) the antecedent phrase, including measures 43 to 46, is begun forte, and a diminuendo is made from the b³ in bar 44 to the c³ in measure 45. The consequent phrase, beginning in measure 47, is initiated quietly, but contrary to bar 44, a crescendo is made in bar 48 to the e³ in bar 49. The remainder of the phrase, to the resolution in bar 51, is played forte.

The phrase group in bars 208 to 217 is also elucidated by dynamic change. In the phrases ending in measures 209 and 211, the dynamics follow the contour of the melodic line, including diminuendos to the final notes. However, on the final phrase of the group, beginning in bar 213, a crescendo is made to the e² flat in bar 214. The e² flat in this bar represents the final note of the preceding phrase group and the beginning of a new phrase. Therefore, an elision occurs in bar 214.

In terms of the overall structure of the movement, the arrival of the B section of the Rondo is reflected by a softer dynamic level and the cultivation of a dolce mood. The first eight bars of the final return of the principal theme of the movement, beginning in bar 334, is initiated according to the principle of equal dynamic treatment for repeated formal sections. This precedent is broken in bar 341, however, when the c³ on the sixth beat is held slightly longer and played louder than the same pitch in bar 6 of the opening statement. The changes commenced in measure 341 are carried further in bar 343, when the third and fourth beats are heavily accented and are played loudly (example 2.53). The increased volume level and accentuation of the two eighth notes is carried out to stress the variation in the two pitches in contrast to previous statements of the phrase.

Example 2.53

343

Hasty's concept of building and releasing tension often tends to create longer phrase units. Three groups of phrases in the Rondo that are affected by this are the short groups from bars 91 to 97, 99 to 105, and 311 to 318. Each of these sections is comprised of a number of short phrases that have greater continuity when treated as parts of a single lengthy succession.

The individual measures from bars 91 to 96 (example 2.44) constitute an accumulation of tension that is released upon the resolution of the harmonic structure in bar 97. Therefore, a crescendo is made from measures 91 to 96, and the individual measures are interpreted as parts of a large structure. In the same manner, Hasty interprets measures 99 to 101 and 103 to 105 as further extensions of the tension that has developed in the six bars preceding bar 97. Measures 311 to 317 comprise an accumulation of tension that is not released until bar 318. This interpretation precludes the tendency to divide the section into four or five individual short phrases.

As in the Allegro, effects produced by dynamic change include grazioso moods, changes of character within individual phrases, and echoes. Included in the category of echoes are exact repetitions of material and quasi echoes in short subsequent groups that are not exact repetitions of preceding material.

Measure 86 (example 2.49) is identical in notation to measure 84; therefore, it is played as an echo of bar 84. To facilitate this echo, Hasty changes the dynamic level from the piano indication in the Breitkopf and Haertel edition to mezzo piano. Since bars 228 and 229 are identical to bars 226 and 227, they are also performed as an echo. Unlike a number of interpreters of the Rondo, Hasty does not make a change of dynamics in measure 143, even though the measure is a reiteration of measure 142 (example 2.54). This is probably to maintain the lyricism and dynamic direction of the passage.

Example 2.54

Quasi echoes occur in bars 88, 170, 172, and 309. Each of these measures is either an outgrowth of preceding material and therefore similar in nature to another passage, or is set apart in such a way as to warrant a sudden lowering of dynamics to create an echolike effect.

Bar 88 (example 2.40) begins an octave higher than bar 86 but has identical pitches in its first three sixteenth notes. It therefore possesses characteristics that permit it to be performed as an echo. Measures 309 and 310 are comprised of pitches that are an octave lower than the pitches in measures 307 and 308 (example 2.55). Bar 307 is consequently initiated loudly, and the second half of bar 309 is performed quietly.

Example 2.55

The interjected low notes in bars 344 and 345 (example 2.56) are played piano. The sudden change in dynamics from the forte level of the surrounding marcato pitches gives the low notes a grazioso quality. An additional benefit derived from this interpretation is better intonation for the low notes. The low f^1 and g^1 in bars 344 and 345 will not be as flat if played piano as they would be at the forte level indicated by the Breitkopf and Haertel edition. The melody outlined by the a^3 and b^3 of bars 344 and 345 and the c^3 of bar 346 will also be more predominant.

Example 2.56

Character change within individual phrases is the result of modification of the dynamics in bars 160 and 208. The placement of a piano marking on the second sixteenth note of bar 160 transforms the phrase from marcato to grazioso. As illustrated in example 2.57, the grazioso character of the phrase is maintained in measures 161 and 162 by playing the two interjected low notes softly, in a spaced and accented fashion. A similar change of character is the result of an alteration in dynamics from marcato forte in bar 207 to piano in bar 208.

Example 2.57

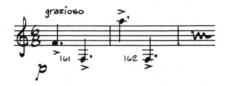

In interpreting dynamics in the concerto, Hasty considers changes of volume not only as an integral part of phrasing and as a means for the production of effects, but in terms of the interaction between the solo and tutti parts and the interaction and balance between the clarinet and orchestra. It is his opinion in general that tuttis should not be marked at higher dynamic levels than surrounding material in the solo part. He also believes that solo parts must match the dynamic levels of the tuttis that precede them.

The dynamic level of the orchestra part is adjusted in bars 46 and 186 of the Rondo in order to match more closely the volume level of the preceding solo material. In measure 46 the level is altered to piano, and in measure 186 the tutti begins softly and crescendoes to forte. The piano entrance in bar 186 constitutes a change from the subito forte that is indicated in the Breitkopf and Haertel edition. Hasty raises the dynamic level in bar 51 to forte to match the volume of the clarinet part in the preceding section. The dynamic level of the clarinet part is also raised in bars 43 and 187 to match the volume level of the tutti sections that anticipate them.

To improve the balance between the solo and tutti parts, the volume in bars 65 to 68 is raised from the piano direction in the Breitkopf and Haertel edition to mezzo forte. This change in dynamic level is necessary to improve the audibility of the clarinet part, which is written in a low *tessitura* in these measures.

As in the Allegro and Adagio movements, Hasty includes quasi cadenzas and ritardandos that are not indicated in the Breitkopf and Haertel edition. Each of the quasi cadenzas appears at a point in which there is either a rest in the orchestra part, as in bar 159, or a rhythmic pulse on the second through sixth beats, as in bars 160 and

207. The quasi cadenza in bars 159 to 160 is performed with a slight elongation of the time value of the b³ flat that crosses the two bars and a return to the original tempo by the end of the second of the two measures. In bar 207, the skip that includes the c² and c³ is played more slowly than the established rhythm.

The ritardandos that are added in measures 219 and 221 are a modification of the ritardandos that most performers add to this passage. In Hasty's interpretation a slight ritardando is executed by the orchestra in the first five beats of bar 219, which is a part of the tutti appearing in bars 218 and 219. A fermata is placed over the eighth-note rest on the sixth beat of bar 219, thus bringing the rhythm to a complete halt. The motion resumes in measure 220 with the solo part as the predominant line. The tempo in bar 220 is slightly slower than the original tempo. Another ritardando occurs on the first four beats of bar 221, before the tempo is again resumed in bar 222.

In addition to a cessation of the rhythmic pulse in the quasi cadenza passages (a factor that increases the listener's awareness of the rhythm of the movement), the rhythmic element of measures 332 and 333 is alternately emphasized and deemphasized. The syncopation that occurs in bar 332 is stressed by tonguing and accenting the c² sharp pitches on the second and fourth beats. Contrarily, the second beat of bar 333 is begun pianissimo, and a crescendo is made through the remainder of the bar. The initiation of the second beat at a quieter dynamic level and the crescendo that follows tend to deemphasize the syncopation and carry the line toward bar 334.

An interesting feature of Hasty's interpretation of the ornamentation of the movement is his treatment of the trills. Both inverted and noninverted trills are utilized in the Rondo. Each of the inverted trills, in bars 50, 177, 296, and 321, and one noninverted trill, in bar 90, is preceded by a pitch lower than that of the trilled note. The remaining trills in the movement, in bars 315 and 317, which are performed as noninverted trills, are preceded by pitches that are higher than the trilled notes. It therefore must be concluded that the only criterion that Hasty uses in determining the posture of the trills in the movement is the sound of each individual trill.

Changes of notation from the Breitkopf and Haertel edition are made in measures 169, 205, and 311 to 313 of the Rondo. As shown in example 2.58, the a¹ on the fourth beat of bar 169 is changed to a b¹ flat. This allows the series of intervals in bar 169 to conform to the succession of intervals in bars 171 and 173. In measure 205 (example 2.59) an a^1 flat grace note is added to precede the fourth beat. This causes measure 205 to conform to the pattern established in bars 197, 200, and 203 of the tutti part.

Measures 311 to 313 are not transposed downward an octave, although that is done by other interpreters of the concerto. It is Hasty's opinion that the passage was originally written an octave lower for an instrument that possessed a low c. Since the range of modern clarinets does not include low c, the entire passage from bar 311 to 313 is transposed upward an octave in the Breitkopf and Haertel edition and should be performed as written.

Example 2.58

Example 2.59

THREE

Robert Marcellus's Interpretation

Robert Marcellus's approach to the Clarinet Concerto is based on a lifetime of study of the piece, as well as on a thorough familiarity with Mozart's other works. He has acquired much of his knowledge of the concerto through his performances of the work under some of the world's finest conductors, including Lorin Maazel, Louis Lane, Thor Johnson, Pablo Casals, Robert Shaw, and George Szell.

For imparting knowledge about the concerto, Marcellus gives the greatest amount of credit to the late George Szell, former conductor of the Cleveland Orchestra. Marcellus performed the work with Szell during the 1955 season of the Cleveland Orchestra and again in the 1960–61 season. Later he recorded the work with that organization.

Marcellus is emphatic in his belief that the concerto represents more than a beautiful work for the clarinet. In his view the work represents the mature, almost final work of a genius; it is not merely a tour de force for the display of technique. This view ranks the Mozart Clarinet Concerto as different in character from, for example, Weber's concerti for clarinet. Marcellus believes that Mozart's Clarinet Concerto must not be the victim of clarinetistry and technique; rather, the legato aspects of the work, along with the evenness of tone, should receive emphasis in its interpretation.

In Marcellus's approach to the concerto, the warmth of the Central European concept of Mozart, transmitted to the artist by Szell, has great influence on the handling of phrasing and technical factors such as articulation. Marcellus stresses that the melodic time must be fully granted; that is, the melody must not be forced ahead too quickly.

The basis of Marcellus's present interpretation of the concerto was formed during the 1955 season of the Cleveland Orchestra, as the result of a discussion with Szell. According to Marcellus, after a rehearsal of the concerto Szell commented that Marcellus might have used too much articulation in the work. Later in the discussion Szell asked Marcellus to consider what view of the concerto would result if the work were equated in its style with Mozart's Clarinet Quintet (K. 581). After further study of the concerto, Marcellus concluded that definite parallels exist in the styles of the two works. He then modified his playing of the concerto to follow more closely the mood and style of the quintet.

Two of the interpretive elements that Marcellus changed to achieve a closer correlation between the concerto and the quintet are phrase structure and articulation. In each of the three movements of the concerto, short phrases are frequently combined to create longer, more expansive phrases, and articulated notes are given added length (rather than being performed *secco*) and are slurred at times in order to duplicate more closely the broad lines of the quintet.

It is Marcellus's belief that articulations are nothing but phonetics; they are consequently devices that one uses to increase his musical vocabulary. Marcellus therefore places particular importance on the length of separated notes, and says that in order to produce the large variety of gradations of duration of separated pitches necessary for performance on the clarinet, one must utilize many tonguing sylla-bles. He uses syllables of the tongue that range from *d* or *t* to *th* and *the*. In interpretive decisions regarding the length of articulated notes, his opinion is that the length of separated pitches does not always correspond with the tempo or dynamic level at which they are performed.

As a general pattern in Marcellus's approach to the phrase structure of the concerto, the typical change in character within a Mozartean phrase is stressed. In explaining the change of character that takes place within a single phrase, Marcellus paraphrased Erich Leinsdorf, citing the conductor as recognizing the wonderful variety of character within one phrase of Mozart's work: the first half of the phrase is often sustained and espressivo, and the second half often ends brilliantly. According to Marcellus, Szell also pointed out this change of character when he noted that one of the inherent traits of

Mozart's music is that the composer allows one to speak expressively and then in a brilliant fashion. An example of such a change of character is found in the opening theme of the Allegro movement of Mozart's Symphony no. 39 in E-flat Major. It must be noted that Marcellus's concept of brillante or con brio playing is somewhat tempered when it appears in the Mozart Clarinet Concerto. In the context of the concerto, brillante, or con brio, signifies a part of the phrase that is slightly animated, but not agitato.

As is the case with Hasty's work, the harmonic background of the concerto is an important factor in Marcellus's interpretation. In each of the three movements the modulations, altered harmonies, chordal progressions, and nonharmonic tones are not only considered in interpretive decisions, but are often stressed to bring them to the listener's attention.

In his approach to dynamic phrasing within the work, Marcellus is continually aware of the building and releasing of tension that occurs within phrases. He theorizes that the accumulation of tension within a phrase should be released in conjunction with the resolution of dissonance in the harmony in the cadence at the end of the phrase, an idea similar to Hasty's concept of tension and release.

Marcellus deals with trills and *rubati* in much the same fashion in each of the three movements. In his interpretation of the work almost all trills are initiated from the note above the written pitch of the trill. When rubato is utilized, it is ruminative in nature.

ALLEGRO MOVEMENT

A further magnification of Marcellus's philosophies concerning his view of Mozart's Clarinet Concerto can be found in his approach to the Allegro movement, particularly in the rendition of the melodic line, influence of the harmonic background, phrase structure, dynamic phrasing, articulation, and alteration of notation.

The characteristic change that takes place within Mozart's melodic lines, as observed by Leinsdorf and Szell, is the focal point of the manner in which Marcellus treats the melodic line of the Allegro. The first appearance of the change of mood in the line from espressivo to poco brillante is in bars 62 and 63 (which are identical to 256 and 257 of the recapitulation). As illustrated in example 3.1, the eighth notes on the first beat of bar 62 are played espressivo, and the sixteenth notes of bar 63 are performed poco brillante. A similar occurrence of this fluctuation in the mood of the line appears in bars 78 to 80 and identically in bars 272 to 274 of the recapitulation. As shown in example 3.2, bars 78 and 79 are played dolce, in an espressivo fashion, followed by the brillante sixteenth notes on the first beat of bar 80.

Marcellus interpolates a slight decrease in the tempo of bar 198, followed by a return to tempo in the second half of bar 199 (example 3.3), which tends to create an effect similar to the change from espressivo to brillante. All of measure 198 and the first half of measure 199 are performed in a contemplative manner. The gradual return to the original tempo on the second half of bar 199 produces a feeling of a quickening of tempo that invokes the same effect as the brillante treatment.

Example 3.1

Example 3.2

Example 3.3

Passages in which espressivo and brillante playing are utilized but not directly opposed occur in bars 82 and 83, 112 and 113, and 69 to 75. According to Marcellus, measure 82 (example 3.4) must be played in a reflective manner with *tenuto* effects on each of the triplets for optimum musical meaning. He also considers bar 83 to be a variation of bar 82 and believes that it should be performed in a similarly reflective manner. In order to create a more ruminative mood in bar 83, Marcellus slurs the entire measure. Bars 112 and 113 are also performed in a contemplative manner. As shown in example 3.5, the tempo of these two measures slows down slightly; the original tempo is resumed in measure 114, thus creating a *brillante* effect. Measures 69 to 75 provide an example of a passage in which a con brio section is not preceded by espressivo material. Beginning with the sixteenth notes on the first two beats of bar 69, the passage is played con brio, with the articulations and dynamics as indicated in the Breitkopf and Haertel edition.

Example 3.4

Example 3.5

Features of the harmonic background of the Allegro that are stressed in Marcellus's performance include nonharmonic tones, modulations, and the harmonic progression. In the Allegro these harmonic devices often determine the location of inflections in the melodic line and create points of arrival for dynamic direction.

Nonharmonic tones, such as the *appoggiatura* on the first eighth note in bar 58 and subsequent appearances of the principal theme, at times determine the position of expressive inflections in the melodic line. The a^3 in bar 58 (example 3.6) becomes the focal point of the two-measure phrase that has its beginning in bar 57. The *appoggiaturas* on the first beats of measures 173 and 177 also become successive points of emphasis in the two phrases beginning in bars 172 and 176.

A modulation in the Allegro that is specifically noted by Marcellus occurs in bars 81 to 85. Marcellus believes that the material in these measures must move toward the cadence that occurs in the first half of bar 85 and that it is necessary for bar 84 to move dynamically in the same direction. The perfect authentic cadence in bar 85 confirms the tonality of C major (concert pitch), which begins in bar 81.

An example of a harmonic progression in the Allegro that is stressed by Marcellus occurs in bar 143. According to his view, bars 141 and 142 have the first beat of bar 143 as their point of arrival. Analysis of the chordal structure of these three measures reveals tonic and tonic seventh harmonies in measures 141 and 142, respectively, and a change to subdominant harmony in bar 143. The tonic chord with an added seventh in bar 142 functions as a secondary dominant, creating harmonic tension that is resolved on the first beat of bar 143.

In accordance with his belief that the phrase structure of the concerto should be as expansive as possible, Marcellus combines a number of short phrase groups in the Allegro to make single phrases. In measures 57 and 58, 100 to 102, and 172 to 176, phrases of one measure or less are combined for greater length. A slur is placed over measures 57 and 58 (example 3.6) to ensure that the g^3 on the first two beats of measure 57 will be included as part of the single phrase encompassed by the two measures. In a similar manner, the short phrase included in bar 172 and the first beat of bar 173 (example 3.7) is slurred to the remaining material in bar 173 in order to create a more expansive single phrase, which ends after the second beat of bar 176. The melodic line in bars 100 to 102, shown in example 3.8, is carried in a manner that connects the three short one-measure phrases, thereby making them parts of a longer phrase that includes bars 100 to 105. Marcellus accomplishes this expansion by not slighting the rhythmic value of the last eighth note in each of the three bars and by making a gradual diminuendo throughout the succession. The diminuendo replaces crescendos and diminuendos within each of the individual measures.

Example 3.6

Example 3.7

Example 3.8

Another interesting feature of Marcellus's approach to the phrase structure of the Allegro is his recognition of the formal elisions that occur in bars 87, 89, and 90 (example 3.9). In each of these measures the eighth note on the second half of the first beat serves as both the beginning of a new phrase and the second of a group of two eighth notes that begins on the first beat. Marcellus articulates each of the transitional eighth notes in these measures to make the elisions more evident to the listener. The groups of two eighth notes are not divided by slurring from the second to the third eighth notes as they are in some performances of the Allegro.

Example 3.9

As with the elisions, a number of phrases in the Allegro are carried across bar lines. Such phrases occur in bars 90 to 92 and 190 to 192. The phrase beginning on the second eighth note of bar 90 ends on the c^2 sharp in the first beat of the succeeding measure (example 3.10). A subsequent phrase then begins on the second beat of bar 91 and concludes with the c^1 sharp on the first beat of bar 92. To ensure that the c^1 sharp in bar 92 will be heard as a part of the previous phrase,

Marcellus adds a slur from the preceding d^1 on the fourth beat of bar 91. A similar phrase construction is found in measures 190 and 191, as illustrated in example 3.11. While the a^1 on the first beat of bar 190 is part of the preceding phrase, the remaining material in the measure is a part of another phrase, which ends with the e^1 on the first beat of bar 192. No alterations are made in the articulations of this passage as they appear in the Breitkopf and Haertel edition.

Example 3.10

Example 3.11

Marcellus's approach to dynamic phrasing in the Allegro is a reflection of his concept of the style of the concerto as broad and expansive. To create the effect of expansive phrases and to build a feeling of continuity, he often uses a form of sequential dynamic phrasing in which subsequent phrases of phrase groups are performed at higher or lower dynamic levels than the phrases that precede them. Marcellus also utilizes sequential dynamic phrasing to stress increasing tensions and directions in the melodic line.

Measures 108 to 110, 145 to 147, 184 to 186, 210 to 213, and 334 to 336 of the Allegro, shown in examples 3.12 to 3.16, are comprised of sequences of one-measure phrases in which the dynamics grow louder in a terraced fashion with each measure. Measures 108 to 110, 145 to 147, and 334 to 336 constitute groups of three short phrases, and measures 210 to 213 are comprised of a series of four short phrases. The first three phrases of the latter series are one measure or less in length and the fourth phrase three measures long.

Example 3.12

Example 3.13

Example 3.14

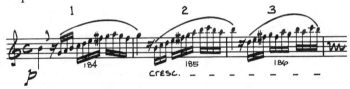

Example 3.15

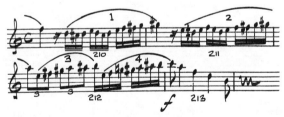

Example 3.16

Passages in which lengthy diminuendos occur include bars 143 and 144, 331 to 333, and 339 and 340 (examples 3.17 to 3.19). Interestingly, the short sequential passages that utilize diminuendos occur in descending successions of phrases. Since Marcellus increases volume in the descending sequence in bars 108 to 110, however, a prescribed pattern for dynamic changes of this nature does not appear to exist. The elongated diminuendo, which is a more subtle device than terraced dynamics, produces a subsiding of dynamic tension in each of these passages.

Example 3.17

Example 3.18

Example 3.19

In the interpretation of dynamic change in the Allegro movement, as well as in the Adagio and Rondo movements, changes in volume levels in short reiterated phrases are not considered imperative by Marcellus. Bars 182 and 183, which are a repetition of bars 180 and 181, make up the only passage in the Allegro in which he might lower the volume level on an immediate reiteration (example 3.20). It is his general opinion that dynamic changes on repetitions are made only because they sound good, and are not based on other musical elements for justification.

Example 3.20

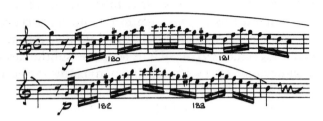

As mentioned previously, Marcellus avoids a *secco* staccato in all articulated passages of the concerto. In his performance of the work he continually strives for a more melodic style of staccato. Specific examples of passages in the Allegro that are articulated as indicated in the Breitkopf and Haertel edition are found in bars 69, 73, and 103 (and also in bars 263, 267, and 291 in the recapitulation). He believes that in each of these passages the tongued sixteenth notes must have breadth and must not be played too short.

Additional insight into Marcellus's method of tonguing can be gained by examining his approach to the articulated eighth notes in bar 94. He feels that these three eighth notes must be separated, but not too widely spaced. He accomplishes this by letting the attack of each successive eighth note stop the preceding one (in this case, without relaxation of wind pressure). Marcellus credits Daniel Bonade for having taught him this method of staccato tonguing.

With the exception of bar 130 (example 3.21), where the eighth notes on the second beat are tongued in order to conform to the articulations of the first violin part in the preceding measure, articulation changes in the Allegro consist of the addition of slurs. Diatonic successions of sixteenth notes of one and two measures and arpeggios comprised of sixteenth notes are frequently slurred rather than tongued as indicated in the Breitkopf and Haertel edition.

Example 3.21

The sixteenth-note runs in bars 141 and 142, and in 180 and 181 and 182 and 183 of the Allegro (examples 3.22 and 3.20) each encompass two measures; the run phrases are entirely slurred in each case. The one-measure succession of sixteenth notes in measure 329 is also slurred by Marcellus. Use of the tongue is eliminated in the arpeggios that occur in bars 83 and 84 (example 3.4) and in bars 146 and 147 (example 3.13). Each of these arpeggios encompasses two beats and is tongued on the lowest pitch.

Example 3.22

In addition to the changes in the rhythmic pulse of the movement that occur on the fermatas in bars 127 and 315, Marcellus allows a slight slowing of the tempo in two passages where he interprets the melodic line in a more contemplative manner. The tempo in bars 112 and 113 (example 3.5) is reduced as the phrase becomes more ruminative and is regained by the middle of bar 114. In like manner, a slight reduction in tempo is made in bar 198 and is then followed by an accelerando to the original tempo in the middle of bar 199 (example 3.3).

Notational changes in the Allegro are minimal in Marcellus's interpretation. As in Hasty's interpretation, the third and fourth beats of bars 146 and 147 are raised an octave (example 3.13). Unlike Hasty, Marcellus does not raise the first two beats of the measure 333 an octave. It is also his belief that the diminuendo included in bars 331 to 333 is more effective if bar 333 is performed as written in the Breitkopf and Haertel edition.

ADAGIO MOVEMENT

Marcellus believes that the primary clue to the interpretation of the Adagio is seen in the second and third beats of bar 81. He credits Szell with pointing out the reharmonization on the second beat in the orchestral part beneath the sustained g^3 in the first violin as evidence of the introspective, contemplative nature of the second movement.

This reharmonization, a subdominant chord with a flatted third, creates the molto espressivo mood that must pervade the entire movement. A similar, but less forceful, reharmonization takes place in measure 22 beneath a sustained b³ flat in the clarinet part. The harmony introduced on the second beat of this measure is a dominant chord in its second inversion. As might be expected, in Marcellus's interpretation of the Adagio one of the most expressively played measures is measure 22 (example 3.23). The succeeding measure is performed in a contemplative manner.

Example 3.23

Marcellus's treatment of the grace notes that occur before the third beats of bars 7, 15, 23, and 86 of the solo part in the Adagio is also an interesting feature of his interpretation. He performs the grace notes on the third beats and slightly out of rhythmic context, not allowing them a duration equal to the sixteenth notes on the last quarter of the beats. Marcellus believes that the grace notes can sound overly schooled or pointed if they are performed in measured rhythm. He also observes that the grace notes appear in a work written late in Mozart's career, near the beginning of the romantic period. Therefore, it is also possible to perform them ahead of the beat, as grace notes were played in the romantic era.

In Marcellus's words, the movement becomes "more plastic" in the section that includes measures 33 to 59. As in Hasty's interpretation, Marcellus performs this section (the B section of the formal structure) with greater flexibility in the rhythmic pulse.

No other changes are made in the rhythm of the Adagio until the final note of the clarinet part is reached. The final pitch in the solo part is sustained one extra beat beyond the written quarter note. Unlike many performers, Marcellus proceeds directly from the cadenza in bar 59 to the principal theme in bar 60.

With the exception of only a few measures, the dynamic levels in Marcellus's interpretation correspond to the markings in the Breitkopf and Haertel edition. As illustrated in example 3.24, the diminuendo in bar 84 is eliminated, and bar 85 is performed poco *più* piano. Thus bar 85, which is a reiteration of the material in bar 84, sounds like an echo. The diminuendo in bar 88 is also eliminated, and the passage is performed more gently than the preceding phrase.

Example 3.24

Marcellus performs the return of the principal theme in bar 60 at the pianissimo level indicated in the Breitkopf and Haertel edition. Even though he uses a higher dynamic level for this passage than the *sotto voce* utilized by Hasty, the basic concept of calling the listener's attention to the return of the initial formal section is the same.

In addition to recognizing the beginning of the B section of the formal structure in bar 33 and the return of the A section in bar 60, Marcellus considers the material from bar 83 to the end of the Adagio as a coda. He therefore develops a framework of dynamic phrasing that allows the section to become gradually more and more quiet. This creates an effect of settling down.

For his cadenza in the Adagio, Marcellus quotes the cadenza that Mozart wrote for his Clarinet Quintet (K. 581); as is illustrated in example 3.25, Marcellus's cadenza for the concerto duplicates the cadenza in the Adagio movement of the quintet. By using the quintet cadenza Marcellus strengthens the association between the two works.

Example 3.25

Marcellus makes no changes in the notation or articulation of the Adagio. Unlike Hasty, Marcellus does not change the notation of bar 74 to match the pitches of bar 23 in the A section of the movement.

RONDO MOVEMENT

Marcellus's interpretation of the melodic line of the Rondo is often similar to his treatment in the Allegro. As in the Allegro, he frequently establishes a change of character from dolce or espressivo to poco brillante or con brio within individual phrases. As in his rendition of the Allegro, certain pitches in the melodic line are performed more expressively than the pitches that surround them.

Phrases in the Rondo that adhere to the pattern of espressivo to brillante occur in bars 5 and 8 (and also in bars 252 and 253 and 272 and 273 in subsequent appearances of the principal theme), 36 to 38, and 48 to 50. As is illustrated in example 3.26, measures 5, 6, and 7 are performed espressivo, quasi-dolce, and con brio, respectively. Bars 36 and 37 (example 3.27) are also played expressively and then are complemented by a succeeding measure that is performed con brio at a louder dynamic level ("poco dynamics," in Marcellus's terminology). A similar interpretation is given the passage in bars 48 to 50 (example 3.28); however, the poco brillante counterpart of the phrase is performed in a dynamically understated manner.

Example 3.26

Example 3.27

Example 3.28

For added expressiveness *tenuto* effects are included on the eighth notes in measures 334 and 336 and over the dotted quarter note in measure 339. The increased duration given these pitches permits them to be performed in a more expressive manner. For example, the b³ in bar 339 is played molto espressivo, thus rendering it the focal point of the expressiveness of the Rondo movement (example 3.29).

Example 3.29

The harmonic background of the Rondo is also occasionally stressed in the solo part. As in the Allegro, Marcellus utilizes added duration and dynamic change to highlight harmonic progression, altered chords, and nonharmonic tones. Passages where changes in the harmonic progressions are stressed include bars 17 and 18, 19 and 20, and 36 and 37. The change from dominant harmony in bar 17 to tonic harmony in bar 18 is accentuated by the use of a crescendo in the second half of bar 17 in the solo part and *tenuto* playing on the c² on the first beat of the succeeding measure (example 3.30). In a similar fashion, the change from the secondary dominant sonority in bar 19 to the dominant chord in bar 20 is stressed by a crescendo in bar 19 and a *tenuto* effect on the first beat of bar 20. Additional emphasis through articulation is provided for the g³ on the first beat of bar 20. In each of these two passages a diminuendo is made after the change of harmony is highlighted.

Example 3.30

Marcellus also emphasizes the nonharmonic tone on the first beat of bar 37 through a crescendo in bar 36 and *tenuto* performance of the c^2 sharp on the first beat of bar 37. As with the accentuated harmonic progressions, he carries out a diminuendo in the remainder of bar 37 after stressing the *appoggiatura* on the first beat.

When not utilized in conjunction with espressivo playing and emphasis on the harmonic background, Marcellus's choice of dynamics in the Rondo is often influenced by his interpretation of the formal structure of the movement. Dynamic changes are used to create long, expansive phrases and to illuminate short repeated phrases or returns of large formal sections.

As in the Allegro, Marcellus uses sequential dynamic phrasing in the Rondo to create longer phrases. The longest sequential passages in the movement occur in measures 105 to 110 and 238 to 243. As is illustrated in example 3.31, the volume level of each of the three smaller groupings in the sequence in bars 105 to 110 is reduced in a terraced manner.

The remaining successions in which dynamic phrasing is interpreted sequentially are comprised of groupings of two phrases. The two phrase groups included in measures 16 to 23 (example 3.30), and 263 to 269 in the return of the principal theme, are performed as a single phrase. As in the larger sequential passages, the dynamic level is raised in the second of the two groups. In the case of measures 16 to 23, this crescendo begins on the sixth beat of bar 18 and concludes on the g^3 in bar 23.

Two other phrase groups that are interpreted in a sequential fashion occur in bars 43 to 51 (example 3.28) and in bars 289 to 297 in the return of the principal theme. Like Hasty, Marcellus plays the first part (measures 43 to 46) piano, and then initiates a diminuendo in bar 44 that extends to the highest pitch of the group in measure 45. A diminuendo is not made at the end of the first part in bar 46; rather, the final note of the passage is carried forward to connect the group to the succeeding material. The subsequent phrase beginning in measure

47, also initiated at the piano level, crescendoes to the peak of the line in measure 49, thus becoming an affirmation of the first group.

Example 3.31

A unique aspect of Marcellus's interpretation of the Rondo is his conception of the material included in bars 327 to 343 (example 3.32) as a single phrase. His treatment of this section combines both his understanding of the overall form of the movement and his attempt to expand the phrase structure of the concerto whenever possible. Marcellus believes that the final return of the principal theme, from measure 334 to the end of the movement, is a codetta and that measures 327 to 333 provide transitional or introductory material that precedes that section.

Example 3.32

In order to distinguish the final return of the principal theme, Marcellus performs bars 334 to 340 of the codetta at a slightly slower tempo and at a soft dynamic level. He prepares for the piano dynamic level of the section by making a diminuendo in bars 331 to 333. After the first eight measures of the codetta, Marcellus regains the original tempo of the Rondo through an accelerando in bars 341 to 343. The entire passage, from measure 327 to 343, is transformed into a single phrase by connecting the material that precedes and follows the return of the principal theme in bar 334.

The repetition of short phrases in the Rondo is made more apparent in Marcellus's interpretation, as in Hasty's, by changing the dynamic levels at which the reiterated sections are initiated. Sudden dynamic changes are made for repeated identical phrases and quasi echoes in which the succeeding material is not the same. Dynamic change is also made for variety.

Repeated phrases consisting of identical melodic lines occur in measures 84 to 87, 141 to 143, and 226 to 229. In the first of these passages, Marcellus changes the piano marking in the Breitkopf and Haertel edition to a higher volume level in order to contrast the repeated phrase, beginning in bar 86, which is initiated at the piano level (example 3.33). In like manner, measures 228 and 229 are played more quietly than the identical phrase that precedes them (example 3.34). The repeated phrases in bars 141 to 143 (example 3.35) provide a contrast to the passages cited above owing to an increase in the volume of the reiterated phrase that begins on the sixth beat of measure 142. In this passage Marcellus plays the repetition of the first phrase more urgently.

Example 3.33

Example 3.34

Example 3.35

In his performance of the Rondo, Marcellus recognizes the quasi echoes that are indicated by dynamic markings in bars 170 and 172 of the Breitkopf and Haertel edition. In each of these measures (example 3.36) the interjected pitches in the upper register of the clarinet, beginning on g^3 and f^3, respectively, are performed softly, as an echo.

Example 3.36

Other formal devices of the Rondo that Marcellus recognizes include phrases that extend across bar lines. Where internal phrases are not clearly indicated in the Breitkopf and Haertel edition—for example, the resolution of trills and groups of pitches that extend across bar lines—he adds slurs to enhance the clarity of the phrase structure. Slurs across bar lines are added to connect trills and the finish notes of trills to the final pitches of phrases in bars 50 and 51 (example 3.28), 96 and 97, 177 and 178, 296 and 297, 321 and 322, and 345 and 346. As seen in example 3.35, the Breitkopf and Haertel edition is altered so that the slurs indicate phrases that are carried across the bar lines of measures 140 to 143.

Marcellus also observes Mozart's use of elision in phrase structure. According to Marcellus, such an elision occurs on the d^2 in the first beat of measure 95. In his interpretation this pitch provides both a resolution for the c^2 sharp in the preceding measure and a beginning for the new phrase that begins on the succession of sixteenth notes in bar 95.

In addition to the decrease in tempo that Marcellus utilizes in the codetta of the Rondo, he deviates from the established tempo of the movement in bars 221 and 222. A *pochissimo* ritard is made in these measures, with a return to the original tempo on the first beat of bar 222.

As he does in the Allegro, Marcellus adds slurs in many passages of the Rondo to achieve a legato effect in the melodic line of the solo part. Slurs are added to the sixteenth-note runs in measures 43 and 49 (example 3.28), 159 and 160 (example 3.37), 174 and 175 (example 3.38), 225 (example 3.39), 289, and 293. Arpeggio passages in bars 69 and 70 (example 3.40), 84 to 86 (example 3.33), and 301 to 306 (example 3.41) are also slurred. The sixteenth notes in measures 311 to 313 (example 3.42) are articulated in groups of two, as Hasty also prefers to do.

Example 3.37

Example 3.38

Example 3.39

Example 3.40

Example 3.41

Example 3.42

The only alteration in the notation of the Rondo is made by Marcellus on the fifth beat of measure 169. The a[1] of the Breitkopf and Haertel edition is changed to a b[1] flat so that the intervallic structure of the measure will correspond to the sequential pattern in measures 171 and 173. As in Hasty's performance, Marcellus plays bars 311 to 313 (example 3.42) as written in the Breitkopf and Haertel edition. Marcellus does not add a grace note a[1] flat before the fourth beat of measure 205.

FOUR

Anthony Gigliotti's Interpretation

Anthony Gigliotti's execution of Mozart's Clarinet Concerto is primarily a product of his own musical thinking developed through training as a student and experience as a clarinetist in professional orchestras. As a student at the Curtis Institute of Music, Philadelphia, Pennsylvania, he studied clarinet with Daniel Bonade. His foremost experience as an orchestral musician has been with the woodwind section of the Philadelphia Orchestra, with which he became the solo clarinetist.

Among the conductors with whom he has performed the concerto are Stanislaw Skrovaczewski and Eugene Ormandy. Gigliotti credits these conductors with providing orchestral accompaniments that have enhanced his interpretation of the work. He recorded the concerto with the Philadelphia Orchestra during the 1960–61 season (the same season that Robert Marcellus recorded the work).

Gigliotti's concepts of tone, finger movement, and articulation have great influence upon his interpretation of the entire concerto. His thoughts regarding these three rudiments of clarinet performance represent what he believes to be a further development of and, in certain instances, a transition from the teachings of Daniel Bonade.

In his conception of clarinet tone, Gigliotti is one of the originators of what he labels "the American school of woodwind playing." According to Gigliotti, the clarinet tone utilized by the American school is a combination of the inherent characteristics of both French and German tone styles on the instrument. The flexible and limpid quality of French clarinet tone is combined with the darker, richer timbre of the German school of tone. Gigliotti contends that Bonade, who introduced the lighter and brighter French tone to American clarinetists, started the trend toward an American style of clarinet tone when he tempered his own concepts of tone to incorporate some of the darker qualities of German tone, which was the predominant style in America at that time.

While Gigliotti's conception of tone represents an attempt to amalgamate the French and German styles, his theories on technique, that is, finger motion, tend to parallel those of French clarinetists. He notes that the French players, as represented by Daniel Bonade, utilize a lighter, less mechanical finger motion than that used by the Germans. The French views on the manner in which the fingers close the tone holes of the instrument are diametrically opposed to the method employed by the Germans, who utilize a hard-striking or popping action by the fingers as they cover the tone holes. The French clarinetists, and Gigliotti as well, press the fingers on the tone holes lightly with just enough pressure to seal them. According to Gigliotti, the hard-striking action of the fingers utilized by German performers results in an explosive sound as the fingers close the tone holes. This must be avoided if one is to achieve a legato effect when slurring pitches. He believes that a light finger motion and a continuous air-stream will result in legato connections between slurred notes.

Gigliotti's philosophies on articulation are much the same as those held by Marcellus. Like Marcellus, he contends that articulation on the clarinet is similar to articulation in speech and that it requires many variations in the positions and syllables formed by the tongue. The variety of articulation in clarinet performance is dependent upon the style and mood of the music that one is playing. Gigliotti believes that he has diverged from the concepts of tonguing taught by Bonade, in which a sharp, clearly defined staccato is produced by moving the fingers while the tongue touches the reed to stop the tone from sounding. It is his opinion that the action of the tongue must be as light as possible. In his words, "One must articulate on the wind," thus producing a more subtle form of articulation than that which results from touching the reed with the tongue to break the air column.

Gigliotti's views on articulation are reflected in the concerto by his choice of varying lengths of staccato for the Allegro and Rondo movements. It also becomes evident through his variation of the patterns of tongued and slurred pitches in the two movements as a means of creating additional variety and interest in the work. Gigliotti performs the staccato pitches in the Rondo with shorter durations than those in the Allegro. He believes that the contrasting mood of the Rondo necessitates a change in the length of its tongued notes. Both the alteration in staccato length between movements and the utilization of articulation for variety and additional interest are employed by Gigliotti in a manner similar to Stanley Hasty.

Articulation also has a bearing on Gigliotti's choice of dynamic phrasing, as well as his approach to technical passages in the work. Legato tonguing is employed in the concerto in conjunction with specific pitches that are performed with heightened expressiveness. Gigliotti uses the term *portamento* to indicate added emphasis of particular notes in the melodic line, instead of the espressivo style utilized by Hasty and Marcellus. Gigliotti's other concepts of dynamic phrasing in the concerto are perhaps not as carefully structured as those of Hasty and Marcellus and are not as subject to generalization. One point, however, is that in lengthy successions of sixteenth notes in the Allegro and Rondo movements, he believes that runs must present a continuum of sound. Therefore, to achieve a greater continuity of tone, he slurs many of the sixteenth-note runs that are marked staccato in the Breitkopf and Haertel edition.

Other portions of his philosophy in regard to the technical passages within the concerto reflect his concepts of finger motion, musical taste, and phrasing. Like Marcellus, Gigliotti states that the concerto must not be performed as a technical tour de force. Technique, he notes, is only a vehicle for the music.

Gigliotti attempts to utilize a finger motion that is as supple as possible, in order to avoid a popping sound that would accentuate individual pitches, especially in successions of sixteenth notes. Passages containing successive sixteenth notes must convey a feeling of vitality and yet be well controlled rhythmically; they must possess sufficient dynamic direction so that individual pitches will not sound isolated and the rhythm of the successions will not be excessively apparent to the listener.

As a means of achieving greater continuity within runs, Gigliotti organizes internal phrase groupings so that they extend across the beats of the rhythmic pulse. In this form of phrasing, illustrated in example 4.1, the groups extend from the second sixteenth note of the initial group to the first sixteenth note of the subsequent group, a pattern of organization that can be utilized for the entire duration of the passage.

Example 4.1

Gigliotti appears to be somewhat unconcerned with the larger elements of the formal structure of the individual movements of the work. However, when large formal elements are recognized in his performance, they are interpreted identically when repeated, as in the performances of Hasty and Marcellus.

In conjunction with formal elements and individual phrases of the concerto, Gigliotti slurs all trills and ending notes of trills to the note of resolution. In most instances this creates phrases that are carried across bar lines. He couples the trills with the resolutions to develop increased continuity within single phrases of the work. All trills in the concerto are also initiated in accordance with Gigliotti's conception of the rule for performing trills of the classical period. According to this rule, if the trill is approached from a lower pitch, it is begun on the written note. If the trill is preceded by a higher note, it is initiated from the note above the written pitch.

ALLEGRO MOVEMENT

The major factors in Gigliotti's interpretation of the Allegro include the approach to the melodic line, phrasing, articulation, dynamics, formal structure, tempo changes, and changes in notation. In his interpretation of the melodic line of the Allegro, Gigliotti incorporates portamento and dynamic phrasing to enhance the expressiveness of the melodic line. He also employs portamento to accentuate pre-dominant intervals in the melodic line of the solo part.

Legato tonguing and added expressiveness in performing the triplets in the third and fourth beats of measures 123 and 124 (example 4.2) and the first two beats of triplets in measure 212 add interest and intensity to the melodic line. The predominant descending arpeggios that are composed of successive major and minor thirds are highlighted by Gigliotti through his use of portamento (as they are accentuated by Hasty). As illustrated in example 4.3, the descending intervals on the first two beats of measures 87, 89, and 90 (and also measures 202, 204, and 205) are stressed. Bars 116 and 120 (example 4.4) also receive additional emphasis.

Example 4.2

Example 4.3

Example 4.4

Dynamic phrasing is utilized by Gigliotti for increased emphasis of the c^2 in measure 60 and the g^2 in measure 62. As in Hasty's performance, a crescendo is initiated in bar 59 (example 4.5) followed by a diminuendo in bar 60, after the c^2 is played. A slight diminuendo is made on the d^2 pitches both times that they are sounded in measure 59 as part of an overall crescendo in the measure. The g^2 on the first beat of bar 62 is stressed by a crescendo in the preceding measure and is followed by a diminuendo after the pitch is sounded. Although the first pitch of bar 62 is highlighted, the intensity is retained throughout the entire measure.

Example 4.5

In the Allegro, Gigliotti utilizes articulation as a device to interject additional variety, brilliance, and character and to impart an increased sense of direction to the melodic line. He adds slurs in a number of passages in the movement where articulation is indicated in the Breitkopf and Haertel edition. This creates greater fullness and continuity in the sound.

Passages in the Allegro where Gigliotti adds articulation for increased diversity include measures 105, 143 and 144, and 146 and 147. In bar 105 (example 4.6), he tongues the second and third triplets of the second beat and the quarter note on the third beat. The fourth sixteenth notes on each of the four beats of measures 143 and 144 (example 4.7) are articulated, as measures 331 to 333 are also. The third and fourth sixteenth notes of beats one and two of bars 145 to 147 (example 4.8) are tongued to create additional variety in the articulation of the movement.

Example 4.6

Example 4.7

Example 4.8

To generate an effect of brilliance and distinction in the phrase that encompasses measures 69 to 75, Gigliotti employs an extremely light but well-defined group of articulations. Bar 69 is tongued as indicated in the Breitkopf and Haertel edition, and articulation is also introduced in the sixteenth notes on the second half of the third beat and in the fourth beat of bar 73 (example 4.9). The interpretation of this passage provides a contrast to the opening phrases, which Gigliotti performs in a less bravura manner. For added character articulation is also introduced on the f^3 sharp and e^3 on the second beats of measures 129 and 130, respectively, as illustrated in example 4.10.

Example 4.9

Example 4.10

Articulation is introduced in a number of passages in the Allegro to enhance the melodic and dynamic direction of the solo line; it also serves to accentuate the linear motion of the solo part. Among other instances, measure 67 (example 4.1) is divided into two groups of sixteenth notes. Articulation is employed to separate the sixteenth notes on the third and fourth beats of measure 186 (example 4.11) into groups of two. With the exception of the first triplet in bar 82, each of the triplets in the measure is tongued to accentuate the changing directions of the line. Like Hasty, Gigliotti moves dynamically in the triplet arpeggios to the a^3 flat pitches on the third beat of measure 82 and the first beat of measure 83. Melodic and dynamic direction in the solo line is also emphasized in bars 119 (example 4.4) and 123 where the g^1 and e^1 on the first and second beats of each respective measure are tongued.

Example 4.11

Most of the changes in articulation that Gigliotti introduces in the Allegro are related to the elimination of tongued pitches. He contends that the space created between notes by articulation results in an undesirable dissipation of sound in some successions of sixteenth notes. Hence he adds slurs to passages that he feels require louder sound. Gigliotti slurs the first two beats of bar 73 (example 4.9) to make the descending arpeggio more forcefully brillante. In like manner, the third and fourth beats of measures 125 (example 4.12) and 326 are slurred for additional dynamic power. Other measures in which two of the pitches are encompassed by an added slur include bar 145 (example 4.8), which reappears in bars 334 and 335 of the recapitulation, and bar 198. In each of these measures the pitch on the third beat is slurred to the subsequent note.

Successions in which the sixteenth notes are slurred in two groups of eight occur in measures 83, 138 to 140, 141, and 180 to 183. While slurs are included in bars 83 and 180 to 183 (example 4.13) primarily for added strength in the passage, bars 138 to 140 (example 4.14) are slurred to produce greater forcefulness and to carry the succession of sound across the high pitches of the arpeggios. The pitches of measure 141 (example 4.15) are also slurred to augment the amount of tone present and to add a sense of vastness to the successive sixteenth notes that continue through measure 142.

Gigliotti introduces slurs that encompass entire measures in bars 142, 327, 329, and 338, as shown in examples 4.15 to 4.18, in order to produce a greater continuum of sound in the sixteenth-note runs.

Example 4.12

Example 4.13

Example 4.14

Example 4.15

Example 4.16

Example 4.17

Example 4.18

In his interpretation of the phrase structure of the Allegro, Gigliotti is primarily concerned with phrases that in concluding continue across bar lines or the rhythmic pulse. He is also interested in attaining increased continuity within internal phrase groupings, as well as building the overall continuity of the phrase structure of the first movement.

Phrases in which pitches are regrouped and organized so that concluding notes are located across the bar line include the phrases in measures 85 to 90, 116 and 117, 120 and 121, and 200 to 208. As illustrated in example 4.3, the second, third, fourth, and fifth groups in the chain of phrases encompassing bars 85 to 90 begin after the first dotted quarter note in the respective measures and are slurred across the bar lines to conclude on the dotted quarter note in the subsequent measures. Similarly, the d^2 sharp pitches that occur on the fourth beats of both measures 116 and 120 are tongued to create short three-note groups that include the first two beats of measures 117 and 121. In these two passages the d^2 sharp is slurred to the first beat of the successive measure (example 4.4). As is done by Hasty and Marcellus, the phrases included in measures 91 and 92, 114 and 115, 184 and 185, 191 and 192, and 206 to 208 are carried across the bar lines in Gigliotti's rendition.

For the development of increased continuity within individual phrases, articulation is eliminated from measures 58, 63, 140, and 252. In bar 58 (example 4.19), which is a part of the opening phrase in the solo part of the Allegro, the eighth notes on the second beat are slurred for greater cohesiveness in the passage. To achieve a similar effect, Gigliotti slurs from the first beat of measure 63 to the conclusion of the phrase on the quarter note on the first beat of measure 64 (example 4.20). Interestingly, he interprets the two eighth notes on the fourth beat of bar 63 and the quarter note in the succeeding bar as extensions of this phrase. He also slurs to the d^1 on the third beat of measure 140 to increase the continuity of the phrase initiated on the first beat of that measure.

Example 4.19

Example 4.20

To heighten the sensation of forward motion within certain phrases in the Allegro, Gigliotti organizes groups of pitches so that they overlap across the rhythmic pulse. Accordingly, in measures 66 and 67 the sixteenth notes are arranged so that the second, third, and fourth sixteenth notes on each beat are coupled with the first sixteenth note of the subsequent beat. This, according to Gigliotti, results in a greater sense of direction in the succession. A similar pattern of overlapping is employed in bars 71 and 72 (example 4.9) in which the second and sixth eighth notes are tongued to produce two groups of eighth notes that extend across the third beat of measure 71 and the first beat of measure 72.

Gigliotti illuminates repetitions in the phrase structure of the Allegro through the utilization of volume changes on reiterated material. In his performance, measure 144 is played piano and is treated as a repeated phrase, despite the fact that it is written an octave lower than the preceding measure. He stresses this particular dynamic change more than Hasty and Marcellus do. As in the interpretations of the latter two clarinetists, however, Gigliotti performs at the piano level bars 182 and 183 (example 4.13), which are an exact repetition of the two preceding bars.

The overall formal structure of the Allegro is made more apparent in Gigliotti's interpretation through the combination of a dynamic change and a slight alteration in the rhythmic pulse in measure 248. Gigliotti introduces a *calando* in the second half of this measure in conjunction with the diminuendo that is already indicated in the Breitkopf and Haertel edition. The original tempo of the movement is regained on the first beat of bar 249. With the exception of the *calando* and the fermatas that are indicated in measures 127 and 315 of the Breitkopf and Haertel edition, Gigliotti initiates no other interruptions or variations in the rhythmic pulse of the movement.

In accord with his rule of performing trills in the classical style, Gigliotti utilizes both inverted and noninverted trills in the Allegro. Unlike Hasty and Marcellus, Gigliotti begins the trills in measures 74, 153, 225, 226, and 268 on the written pitch. The trill in measure 342 is initiated from the note above the indicated pitch.

Changes in the notation of the first movement that are different from changes made by Hasty and Marcellus occur in bars 324 and 325. In this passage Gigliotti changes the b^1 pitches on the fourth beat of measure 324 and the third beat of measure 325 (example 4.21) to a g^1. Gigliotti's performance also deviates from the renditions of Hasty and Marcellus in measures 145 to 147, where the latter halves of the three measures are played loco instead of an octave higher than written. Like Marcellus, Gigliotti performs the first two beats of measure 333 loco rather than transposing them an octave higher.

Example 4.21

ADAGIO MOVEMENT

In his interpretation of the Adagio, Gigliotti focuses much of his attention on the melodic line, elimination of disruptions caused by articulation, phrase structure, dynamic phrasing, and dynamics. His approach to fluctuations in the rhythmic pulse, ornamentation, changes in notation, and the cadenza are also quite important. Much of his attention to the melodic line, articulation, and phrasing in the second movement is directed toward creating a *cantabile* effect. It is Gigliotti's belief that the Adagio movement must be performed on the clarinet as if it were being sung. He attempts to produce a melodic line that is molto legato; to this end he strives to eliminate finger motion that would result in a popping sound as the fingers are set on the tone holes of the clarinet.

Gigliotti's interpretation of the grace notes that embellish the melodic line in measures 7, 23, 66, 74, and 86 represents a different approach from that of Hasty or Marcellus. Gigliotti believes that the grace notes must be performed exactly on the third beat and in the time of a sixteenth note. According to him, the stress falls on the dotted eighth note that follows the grace note. The only other ornamentations in the movement are two trills that he initiates from the note above the written pitch.

Gigliotti adds slurs in a number of passages in the Adagio to enhance the legato effect of the solo line. For example, the two eighth notes on the first beats of measures 2 and 4 (example 4.22) and also measures 61 and 63 are slurred to the quarter notes that follow on the second beats. Similarly, the dotted eighth and sixteenth notes on the first beat of bar 36 are slurred to the quarter note on the subsequent beat, and the sixteenth notes on the first beat of bar 74 are slurred to the succeeding beat of that measure. More expansive slurs occur in bar 45 (example 4.23), where the entire bar is slurred, and in bars 55 and 57 (example 4.24), in which the slurs extend from the quarter notes on the first beats through the thirty-second notes on the second beats.

Example 4.22

Example 4.23

Example 4.24

As in his interpretation of the Allegro, Gigliotti continues a large number of phrases in the Adagio across the bar lines. For increased continuity, the three eighth notes in measure 5 (example 4.22) are slurred to the dotted quarter note in measure 6. Identical articulation occurs in measures 64 and 65. The three eighth notes in bar 6 (example 4.22) are slurred to the half note in measure 7 in a similar fashion (this feature recurs in measures 65 and 66). Bars 42 (example 4.25), 72, and 95 are connected to the dotted quarter notes in each succeeding bar. In performing the sequence that encompasses measures 17 to 24, like Hasty and Marcellus, Gigliotti extends the phrases begun in measures 17 and 19 (and also 68 and 70) over the bar lines to the first quarter notes of the succeeding measures (example 4.26). Other phrases that are extended to the first quarter note of the subsequent measure begin in measures 55, 57, and 94. Finally, the first sixteenth-note triplet of bar 91 is connected to the eighth notes of the succeeding bar by an additional slur.

Example 4.25

Example 4.26

For increased continuity and dynamic direction, Gigliotti regroups the pitches within measure 35. He organizes the thirty-second notes so that the first group includes the first through fifth thirty-second notes of the primary beat. The second group thus commences on the sixth thirty-second note and concludes with the f^1 on the second beat of the measure.

As in the Allegro, Gigliotti highlights identical repetitions in the phrase structure of the Adagio by taking advantage of dynamic change. Bar 85 is performed pianissimo as marked in the Breitkopf and Haertel edition. Like Marcellus, Gigliotti also plays measure 89 pianissimo, even though the reiterated material is an octave lower.

Passages in which Gigliotti modifies the dynamic levels that are indicated in the Breitkopf and Haertel edition include measures 6, 7, 86, and 95. A notable feature of his performance can be observed in measure 6, where he employs a softer dynamic level than that of the preceding material. The piano level is initiated on the three eighth notes of the bar and remains in effect to the end of the phrase in bar 8. Measure 86 is played piano, rather than the pianissimo called for in the Breitkopf and Haertel edition. Interestingly, Gigliotti performs bar 95 *sotto voce* in place of the marked pianissimo.

Gigliotti utilizes dynamic phrasing in the Adagio movement in conjunction with the sequential passages in order to emphasize individual pitches and maintain the intensity of the melodic line. Gigliotti agrees with Hasty and Marcellus on this point insofar as he increases volume levels in a terraced fashion in the three phrases of the sequence encompassing measures 17 to 24 (and also 68 to 75). He also adds diminuendos in the last halves of bars 17 and 19 of that particular passage, within the framework of the stepwise dynamic increase.

Among the passages in which emphasis is placed on a particular note are measures 33 and 34. Here the e^3 on the first beat of measure 34 gains additional importance in the melodic line as the result of a crescendo that is inserted in the preceding measure and a diminuendo that is added after the pitch is begun. Gigliotti notes that the dynamic intensity of the melodic line must not be interrupted by the eighth-note rests that appear in bars 50 and 51. In this passage care must be taken not to lose the intensity or volume of the solo line during the silence of the rests.

With the exception of the cadenza, Gigliotti does not include any fluctuations in the rhythmic pulse of the Adagio. Unlike Hasty and Marcellus, he does not allow the tempo to become more malleable in the B section of the movement, which encompasses measures 33 to 59. Bar 33 (example 4.27) is performed exactly in rhythm with the dotted eighth- and sixteenth-note figures on the first beat receiving exactly three-fourths and one-fourth of the beat respectively. In addition, the two pitches on the first beat of that measure are performed in a *cantabile* manner, moving dynamically toward the second beat.

Example 4.27

Gigliotti does allow fluctuation within the rhythmic pulse of the Adagio movement in the form of *rubato* in measures 41, 47, and 90. Bars 41 and 90 are performed with a slight punctuation after the eighth note on the first beat, but in a less exaggerated manner than that employed by Hasty, especially in measure 90. Gigliotti does include *rubato* in his interpretation of the sixteenth-note triplets in measure 47. As in Marcellus's rendition, Gigliotti plays the final measure of the movement with no ritardando.

For the cadenza in the Adagio, Gigliotti plays the cadenza from Mozart's Clarinet Quintet. His rationale for this choice is that the concerto is a lengthy work, approximately twenty-eight minutes long, and that the concerto already contains a tremendous amount of divergent material. Gigliotti maintains that, because of the brevity of the quintet cadenza and because additional diversity is not necessary, that cadenza is adequate for the concerto.

Gigliotti introduces no changes in the notation of the movement as it appears in the Breitkopf and Haertel edition. Like Marcellus, Gigliotti performs the sixteenth notes on the first beat of measure 74 as indicated, rather than changing the third and fourth pitches in the succession to b^3 flat and g^3 as in Hasty's interpretation.

RONDO MOVEMENT

Like Hasty and Marcellus, Gigliotti develops close relationships between musical elements in his interpretation of the three movements of the concerto. There is a striking similarity between Gigliotti's and Hasty's interpretations of the first phrase in the solo part of the Rondo. Like Hasty, Gigliotti utilizes a legato tongue for a portamento (espressivo) effect on the second and third eighth notes of measure 4 (and measures 117, 250, 273, and 337 in reiterations of the principal theme). He also employs a portamento effect in measures 151 and 152 on the dotted quarter notes and in measure 163 on the fifth and sixth eighth notes (example 4.28).

Example 4.28

Additional punctuation in the melodic line is added in measure 159 in the form of a firm attack on the c^1 on the first beat. For added stress on this note, which initiates a bravura phrase, it is played slightly shorter than the indicated dotted-quarter-note value.

Gigliotti employs dynamic phrasing in his interpretation of the melodic line to increase expression and to stress pitches that are elements of important chordal progressions in the harmonic background. Among the pitches emphasized by crescendos building toward and diminuendos after a particular point are the f^3 on the first beat of measure 2 (example 4.29), the g^3 on the first beat of measure 112 (example 4.30), which is repeated in measures 243 and 244, and the e^4 on the primary beat of measure 295 (example 4.31). As indicated in the Breitkopf and Haertel edition, the diminuendo that succeeds the g^3 in bar 112 is continued through bars 112 and 113 to the return of the principal theme in bar 114. The change of harmony on the first beat of measure 118 is emphasized in a similar manner. Like Hasty and Marcellus, Gigliotti includes a crescendo in his performance of bar 17 and a diminuendo in bar 18 after reaching the c² on the first beat of that bar.

Example 4.29

Example 4.30

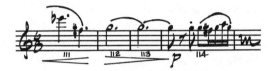

Example 4.31

Gigliotti also employs dynamic phrasing in conjunction with sequential dynamic changes and increased intensity in the solo line. As indicated in the Breitkopf and Haertel edition, the three phrases of the sequence included in measures 105 to 110, illustrated in example 4.32, are initiated at mezzo forte, piano, and pianissimo levels respectively. A crescendo is performed on the first three sixteenth notes of each of the groups in the sequence followed by a diminuendo in the final three sixteenth notes. The dynamic intensity is also increased on the f¹ on the second half of measures 161 and 162 so that the melodic line will retain its intensity through the a³ on the first beat of measure 162 and the c³ on the primary beat of measure 163.

Example 4.32

As in the Allegro and Adagio, Gigliotti groups pitches in the Rondo for an increased sense of direction in individual phrases of the melodic line. The manner in which he arranges the notes in bars 1 and 2, the opening phrase of the final movement, is very similar to Hasty's approach. According to Gigliotti, the two sixteenth note pickups move dynamically to the first eighth note g^3 of measure 1. The second and third eighth notes in this measure move in the same fashion to the a^3 sixteenth note on the fourth beat; then, in turn, the second through the sixth sixteenth notes of the group beginning on the fourth beat move to the f^3 on the first beat of measure 2 (example 4.29). As in a number of the sixteenth-note successions in the Allegro, the sixteenth notes in bars 61 and 62 are organized into groups that overlap across the fourth beat of bar 61 and the first and fourth beats of bar 62 respectively (example 4.33).

Example 4.33

A number of phrases in the Rondo are carried across bar lines to concluding pitches as in the two other movements. The phrase beginning on the fourth beat of measure 45 (example 4.34) is slurred to the quarter note on the first beat of measure 46. For increased continuity, the pitches in bars 82 and 223 are slurred over the bar line to the first eighth note of the subsequent measure. Other phrases that continue across bar lines occur in measures 93 to 95 and 311 to 313. As illustrated in example 4.35, the phrase that begins on the fifth beat of measure 93 concludes with the b^3 flat in measure 94. The c^2 sharp on the fourth beat of measure 94 initiates a new phrase and therefore moves dynamically to the d^2 in the succeeding measure. Finally, in bars 311 to 313 (example 4.36) three short phrases appear that begin on the fourth beat of each measure and end after the second sixteenth note on the third beat of the following measure.

Example 4.34

Example 4.35

Example 4.36

It is Gigliotti's opinion that a shorter style of articulation is utilized for the Rondo than in the two previous movements. He also believes that the length, that is, the spacing, chosen for the three articulated eighth notes in the first half of measure 1 determines the mood of the entire movement. As in the Allegro and the Adagio, many of his deviations from the articulations indicated in the Rondo of the Breitkopf and Haertel edition consist of the addition of slurs to a number of the sixteenth-note successions for increased strength and vigor. Articulation is also utilized in the Rondo to add variety, to separate specific pitches, and to achieve conformity between repeated passages.

Gigliotti adds slurs to all but the first note in many measures in which the Breitkopf and Haertel edition indicates two groups of six sixteenth notes. As is illustrated in example 4.37, all notes but the first sixteenth notes in bars 20, 21, and 22 (and in bars 266 to 268) are slurred rather than articulated as marked. Similarly, for increased sonority, all but the first sixteenth notes of measures 70 (example 4.38) and 284 (example 4.39) are slurred. The sixteenth notes in measures 311 to 313, illustrated in example 4.36, are slurred in two groups of six across the bar lines, beginning with the fourth beat of each measure.

Example 4.37

Example 4.38

Example 4.39

Gigliotti eliminates articulation in lengthy successions of pitches through the use of slurs longer than one measure in certain phrases. In the phrase encompassing bars 6 and 7 (example 4.40), the two sixteenth notes on the sixth beat of bar 6 are included in the slur that spans all the sixteenth notes of bar 7. Gigliotti employs three-measure-span slurs in measures 119 to 121 (example 4.41), and measures 275 to 277 of the recapitulation, 159 to 161 (example 4.42), and 328 to 331. In the latter two passages, the slurs extend across the bar lines to include the final pitches of the phrases.

Example 4.40

Example 4.41

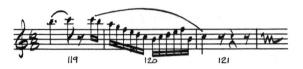

Example 4.42

Groups of sixteenth notes that begin on the first or fourth beats of the measure are frequently slurred in Gigliotti's interpretation of the Rondo. For strength of tone and a bravura effect, slurs are added to the groups of sixteenth notes occurring on the first three beats of bars 61 and 62 (example 4.33) and the groups beginning on the first and fourth beats of measure 69 (example 4.38) and measures 44, 175, and 225.

To maintain maximum interest and diversity in the movement Gigliotti adds slurs in certain passages and deletes them from others. He performs measures 71, 169, 171, and 173 with additional slurs for increased variety. In measure 71, shown in example 4.43, he adds a slur to connect the fourth and fifth eighth notes. Similarly, slurs are introduced to connect the fourth and fifth eighth notes of bars 169 (example 4.44), 171, and 173. In a contrasting manner, articulation is added to his rendition of measures 91, 92, and 93. Contrary to indications in the Breitkopf and Haertel edition, Gigliotti tongues the third through the sixth sixteenth notes and the succeeding two eighth notes in bars 91 and 92 (example 4.45). In measure 93 (example 4.35) he tongues the fourth and fifth eighth notes for increased interest in the passage.

Example 4.43

Example 4.44

Example 4.45

As in Hasty's interpretation, Gigliotti utilizes articulation in several instances in the Rondo to create slight separation between pitches. The outstanding and unique examples of his use of the tongue for separating pitches in the melodic line occur in measures 57 (example 4.46), 65, and 188. In each of these three passages the grace note that appears after the dotted quarter note is articulated to separate it from the eighth note that follows on the fourth beat. It is interesting that while the grace note is written as slurred in these bars, it is marked as articulated in later appearances in the Rondo movement, in bars 197, 200, 215, and 220.

Other pitches that Gigliotti articulates to augment variety in the Rondo include the eighth note that occurs on the sixth beat of measure 58 (example 4.46), as well as in bars 66 and 189, and the eighth notes on the sixth beats of measures 141 and 142 (example 4.47). For improved separation, the tongued c^4 pitches on the sixth beats of bars 141 and 142 are performed slightly shorter than the preceding tongued eighth notes. Gigliotti's employment of articulation in measures 57, 66, 141, and 142 provides a contrast to the interpretations of Hasty and Marcellus, neither of whom employs articulation in these measures.

Example 4.46

Example 4.47

To preserve a measure of uniformity of articulation, Gigliotti articulates recurring passages in the Rondo according to the pattern of their initial appearances. In measure 190 the third and sixth eighth notes are therefore tongued as they were in measures 59 (example 4.46) and 67.

Like Hasty, Gigliotti also employs the tongue or eliminates its use in selected passages to create an improved sense of balance and symmetry. Hence it is his belief that the introduction of a slur in the second group of sixteenth notes in measures 302, 304, and 306 (example 4.48) restores the equilibrium of the passage spanning measures 301 to 307.

Example 4.48

When not employed in conjunction with dynamic phrasing, Gigliotti's alterations of the dynamic levels of the Rondo frequently accompany short reiterated phrase segments and passages in which the volume level of the solo instrument must be adjusted for improved balance and greater sonority of clarinet tone. Unlike Hasty and Marcellus, Gigliotti appears to confine his dynamics changes from the Breitkopf and Haertel edition to sections of the phrase structure that appear identically in immediate repetitions.

Like Hasty and Marcellus, Gigliotti performs the reiterations of the phrases initiated in bars 84 and 226 at a softer dynamic level. The volume level of measure 84 (example 4.49) is changed from the piano marking indicated in the Breitkopf and Haertel edition to a forte so that greater dynamic contrast will result when the phrase beginning in measure 86 is performed piano. According to Gigliotti, the phrase initiated in bar 86 must also be played with less intensity and in a more relaxed manner than the preceding two-measure group. Gigliotti performs measures 228 and 229 piano to accentuate their repetition of the two previous measures. Unlike Marcellus, who performs the reiteration of bars 141 and 142 with greater intensity, Gigliotti plays the repeated phrase, which begins on the sixth eighth note of bar 141, pianissimo.

Example 4.49

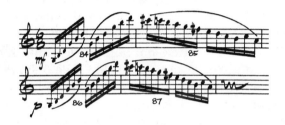

For richer sonority in the low register tone of the clarinet and for improved balance between the solo and orchestral parts, the volume level of the clarinet part is raised in measures 146 and 147, 183 to 186, and 344. Gigliotti performs the pitches beneath the staff in these passages at a forte level to increase resonance and to compensate for the inherent lack of projection of the *chalumeau* register of the clarinet, which is easily covered by other instruments of the orchestra. His rendition of the f^1 on the fourth beat of bar 344, with as rich and sonorous a tone as is possible, provides a direct contrast to Hasty's opinion that this pitch should be performed piano and scherzando.

Gigliotti employs a minimal amount of fluctuation in the rhythmic pulse of the Rondo in order to highlight some of the short repeated phrases and to call attention to the formal structure. In each of the passages in which the tempo is varied, a slight relaxation of the metric pulse occurs.

Like Marcellus and Hasty, Gigliotti performs measures 220 and 221, which form the consequent part of the phrase begun by the tutti in measure 218, at a slightly reduced tempo. In an attempt to stress the approach of new material in the formal development of the Rondo, he introduces a *calando* effect on the fourth through sixth beats of bar 187, as is illustrated in example 4.50. Also like Marcellus, Gigliotti plays measure 333 with a slight reduction in tempo to accentuate the final return of the principal theme in the subsequent measure. However, unlike Marcellus he resumes the initial tempo of the movement in measure 334.

Example 4.50

In accordance with his determination of trills in the entire work, Gigliotti utilizes both inverted and noninverted trills in the Rondo. The trills that appear in measures 96, 315, and 317 are performed from the note above the written pitch, since the indicated pitches are approached from a lower note. Noninverted trills, initiated from the pitch above the written note, occur in bars 50, 177, and 345.

Gigliotti's interpretation of the Rondo necessitates notational changes in only two passages. He changes the fifth eighth note of measure 169 from the a^1 indicated in the Breitkopf and Haertel edition to a b^1 flat, as do Hasty and Marcellus. In contrast to those two performers, Gigliotti performs bars 311 to 313 (example 4.36) an octave lower, with the exception of the c^1 on the second beats of bars 312 and 313. Because there is no c on the standard A clarinet, he substitutes a f^1 for the c in these two measures. He believes that when the passage is performed down an octave, in the *chalumeau* register of the clarinet, it is less awkward technically and is richer sounding. The material that precedes this passage, especially the succession of pitches in measure 310, leads to pitches in the low register of the instrument as well. Gigliotti performs measure 205 as it is written, without an added grace note, as opposed to Hasty.

FIVE

Harold Wright's Interpretation

Harold Wright's interpretation of the Mozart Clarinet Concerto is primarily a product of his own understanding of music and its performance on his particular instrument. He attributes part of his expertise as a clarinetist to his early years of professional experience as a colleague of Marcel Moyse at the Marlboro Music Festival and to the knowledge gained through his study with the late Ralph McLane, a solo clarinetist of the Philadelphia Orchestra who was Wright's only teacher. Before assuming his position as solo clarinetist of the Boston Symphony Orchestra, Wright performed the concerto twice with the Washington National Symphony under two different choral conductors. He does not, however, credit either of the two with giving him any significant insight into the work.

According to Wright, Marcel Moyse, a world-renowned flutist as well as accomplished conductor, influenced many of the musicians that he worked with in the development of more meaningful performances of all kinds of music. Wright comments that Moyse constantly strove to instill life and vitality in the music that he performed. A specific example of a concept advanced by Moyse is the use of articulation to illuminate the features of music rather than as a crutch employed indiscriminately by the instrumentalist to render passages less difficult.

The primary concept of performance of the concerto that Wright attributes to Ralph McLane concerns the tempi of the first and third movements. Wright believes that McLane's preference for lively tempi, especially in the Allegro, was a distinctive feature of his interpretation of the work. According to Wright, the tempo that McLane chose for the Allegro approached 144 beats per minute for the quarter note, which is considerably faster than the metric marking of 104 beats per minute preferred by a number of clarinetists. Wright's own tempo for the Allegro is approximately 120 beats per minute for the quarter note. He states that McLane's tempi for the Adagio and Rondo movements, on the other hand, were not noticeably faster than those chosen by most clarinetists.

In his approach to Mozart's music, Wright follows two general principles. The first, perhaps an outgrowth of his experience with McLane, is that Mozart's works must not be performed too slowly. One of his strong points about the performance of the concerto specifically is a tendency to keep the tempo lively. The second general principle, which becomes increasingly evident in his rendition of the concerto, is his belief that Mozart's music should be performed in a highly romantic manner; that is, in Mozart's music one may take liberties with or make expansions in the tempo to enhance the expressiveness. (This concept is more in keeping with the interpretation of Hasty than it is with the renditions of, for example, Marcellus or Gigliotti.)

Concepts that can be applied to all movements of the work include his belief that the concerto must be performed in a manner that will render it consistently interesting to the listener; moreover, his interpretation of each of the individual movements is subject to change from performance to performance. Marcel Moyse's ideas are reflected in Wright's insistence that the concerto possess diversity through variations in the tone colors, articulations, and dynamics utilized by the player. Interestingly, he is the only performer among those discussed in this book who stresses that his interpretation of the concerto changes slightly with each performance. He emphatically notes, however, that his basic conception of and approach to the work remain constant.

Like many other clarinetists, Wright stresses that the length of articulation is continually varied in the performance of different styles of music. As an illustration of this diversity in the duration of tongued notes, he cites the extremely wide difference in the styles of articulation required for the Nielsen Concerto for Clarinet and the Mozart Clarinet Concerto. He seems to emphasize variations in articulation length within the individual movements of the work to a greater degree than Hasty, Marcellus, or Gigliotti. In the Allegro movement Wright utilizes varied lengths of tongued pitches in order to establish certain moods by the music. One example that he cites illustrates the difference in the durations of the articulations in measures 82 and 87 to 89. In his performance of this passage the triplets in bar 82 (example 5.1) are played with a sharp, percussive style of tonguing, whereas the eighth notes in bars 87 and 89 are executed with a softer, melodically oriented mode of articulation. This manner of playing accords with Wright's concept of a dolce character for the latter two bars.

Example 5.1

In his consideration of the overall formal structure of the individual movements, Wright performs large sections with little variation when they return. This is especially true of his choice of articulations in the reappearances of large segments of the formal structure. One exception to this is his interpretation of the Rondo, where dynamics and articulations are varied in each return of the principal theme.

Another aspect of Wright's interpretation of the concerto that is somewhat subject to generalization is his approach to trills. Most of his interpretive decisions regarding the initiation of trills follow a pattern similar to Gigliotti's rule for trills of the classical period. If a trill is approached from a higher note in the melodic line, Wright begins the trill from the pitch above the written note; conversely, trills approached from a lower pitch in the melodic line are initiated from the indicated note. Like Hasty, Marcellus, and Gigliotti, Wright's primary criteria for the determination of the posture of trilled pitches in the concerto are the resulting sound of the individual trills and the inherent feeling or facility of the finger motions involved in their production.

ALLEGRO MOVEMENT

In his interpretation of the melodic line of the Allegro, Wright emphasizes various devices to enhance expressive qualities and to influence the harmonic background. He frequently employs *tenuto* playing on selected pitches in the solo line to increase expressiveness and to stress the significance of certain notes. In conjunction with the harmonic background of the movement, he places great emphasis on the nonharmonic tones in the melodic line and accentuates them with extended time duration and dynamic phrasing. The harmonic progression of the Allegro is also recognized in his performance.

Exemplary passages in the solo line where Wright employs *tenuto* effects for additional expressiveness include measures 83, 181, and 308. It is of note that each pitch that receives added duration in these measures occurs on the first beat. In bar 83 (example 5.1), the first sixteenth note of the primary beat, an a^3 flat, is performed with added length. Similarly, the c^3 on the initial beat of measure 181 (example 5.2) is sustained longer than its indicated duration. In a manner similar to Hasty's utilization of espressivo devices on successive third intervals in the movement, Wright performs the first and third pitches in measure 308 expressively, with *tenuto* playing on the g^2 sharp and d^2 accompanied by a crescendo on the first beat (example 5.3).

Example 5.2

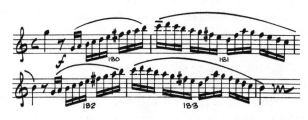

Example 5.3

Wright also introduces *tenuto* effects in bars 140, 146 and 147, and 334 to 336 to emphasize pitches that he believes are crucial to the melodic line. As illustrated in example 5.4, he sustains the g³ on the third beat of bar 140 slightly longer than its allotted time value to highlight it as the highest note in the arpeggio written in that measure. For a similar reason the g⁴ on the third beat of bar 147 is held longer than the quarter note time value indicated in the Breitkopf and Haertel edition. In order to provide a strong, audible bottom pitch for the arpeggios that begin on the first beats of measures 145 to 147 (example 5.5) and measures 334 to 336 (example 5.6), Wright employs *tenuto* performance on the lowest pitches in these measures.

Example 5.4

Example 5.5

Example 5.6

Wright believes that the nonharmonic tones in the solo line of the Allegro are primary generators of interest in the movement. Therefore, he draws attention to a number of them through slight elongation of their time values. He places special emphasis on the *appoggiaturas* in the line, including the g³ sharp on the first beat of bar 67 (example 5.7), as in Hasty's rendition, and the a³ on the initial beat of bar 104 (example 5.8). Other accentuated nonharmonic tones of note are the accented passing tone g³ sharp on the second beat of measure 63, a point of emphasis not found in the interpretations of Hasty, Marcellus, or Gigliotti, and the g^3 sharp on the first beat of measure 305 (example 5.9), which is a suspension that resolves upward in the melodic line.

Example 5.7

Example 5.8

Example 5.9

The harmonic progression of the movement is brought forward in Wright's interpretation through additional emphasis placed on chordal tones contained in the solo line in a number of passages. As in the performances of Hasty, Marcellus, and Gigliotti, the c^2 on the first beat of bar 60, which is a part of the dominant-seventh chordal structure, receives increased support in Wright's rendition as a result of a *tenuto* effect on the note and a crescendo in the preceding measure. Correspondingly, the f^3 on the second beat of measure 62, which is also a member of the dominant-seventh harmony, is accentuated by a crescendo during the eighth notes on the first beat of that measure. The progression of sonorities in bars 216 to 220 is also stressed by a crescendo that extends from the beginning of bar 216 to the e^1 on the first beat of bar 220. To create a more effective crescendo in this passage, the forte volume level indicated in bar 216 of the Breitkopf and Haertel edition is changed to piano.

Wright also broadens the tempo of the Allegro in a number of passages to complement the expressiveness of the solo line. As in Hasty's interpretation, the last three eighth notes of measure 84 are played expansively in Wright's performance. The original tempo is resumed on the first beat of the succeeding measure. In a manner similar to Gigliotti, Wright also broadens the tempo in bar 112 to add greater impetus to the melodic line as it reaches the high point of the phrase that encompasses bars 110 to 114.

Other deviations in the speed of the metric pulse occur in measures 127, 194 to 198, and 315, where fermatas appear in the Breitkopf and Haertel edition. In a mode similar to Hasty, Marcellus, and Gigliotti, Wright initiates the passage beginning on the three quarter notes in bar 194 and extending through the first two beats of bar 198 in a *calando* style. An accelerando to the original tempo is introduced on the triplets in the third and fourth beats of measure 198. The original tempo is regained when the initial beat of the subsequent measure is reached. According to Wright, the sustained pitches indicated in measures 127 and 315 are performed in a style similar to the manner in which a cadenza is prepared. He does not perform either with an exaggerated ritardando.

With the exception of the trill in measure 226, the trills of the first movement are initiated in accord with the pattern of determining trill posture by the pitch that the trill is approached from. Trilled pitches that are preceded by lower pitches in the solo line and therefore are initiated on the written note occur in bars 74, 225 (two trills), and 268. Conversely, the trills in measures 153 and 342 follow higher pitches in the line; hence they commence from the note above the indicated pitch. According to Wright, the trill in measure 226 is begun from the note above, despite its approach in the melodic line from a lower pitch, in order to provide a divergence from the two trills in bar 225, which are initiated from the written pitch.

In his interpretation of the phrase structure of the Allegro movement, Wright devotes much of his attention to the continuity of phrases that extend across the bar lines and to the illumination of the inherent changes of character within certain individual phrases. The phrases that extend through bar lines to their conclusions are given careful attention by Wright, as they are by Gigliotti. Interestingly, unlike Hasty, Marcellus, or Gigliotti, Wright does not employ slurs to connect the ending pitches of phrases, including the resolutions of trills, when they are separated from the preceding material by a bar line. He utilizes a very light stroke of the tongue in place of an added slur. In a manner similar to that of Marcellus, he recognizes the diversity of character that often exists within a single Mozartean phrase and attempts to accentuate changes of mood when they appear.

It is Wright's belief that many phrases in the Allegro are arranged so that they continue across the bar lines to their terminations, rather than ending within the bounds of individual measures. Among the phrases that extend through bar lines are the groupings contained in measures 85 to 94 (example 5.10) and 206 to 209. The passage that encompasses bars 85 to 94 contains seven short phrases that extend over bar lines to their concluding pitches. The first grouping in the series is the longest, extending from the three eighth notes in bar 85 through the dotted quarter note in bar 87, and each of the three successive phrases begins after a dotted quarter note and ends after a dotted quarter note in the subsequent measure. Both of the final two phrases of the succession commence with half notes, on the second beats of bars 91 and 92, respectively. All articulations indicated in the Breitkopf and Haertel edition are followed in this passage. The three short phrases included in measures 206 to 209 are similar to the groupings in measures 91 and 92 in that they begin on the second beats of successive measures. Wright follows the articulations indicated in the Breitkopf and Haertel edition at this point as well and therefore tongues the d^1 sharp in measure 207 and the c^1 sharp in measure 209.

Example 5.10

The phrase encompassing bars 78 to 85 in the A minor section of the principal theme is an exemplary passage in which Wright accentuates a change of character within a single group of pitches. The material included in measures 78 to 80 is performed in a dolce manner. Conversely, the solo line is transformed into a brillante statement in bars 81 to 83, before it becomes more expansive in character in bar 84, and concludes in a dolce temperament, as it began.

In a manner similar to Hasty's interpretation of the phrase beginning in measure 100, Wright introduces a transformation of character on the sustained pitch in this passage. He believes that the d^2 represents both the termination of the preceding phrase and the beginning of the subsequent phrase. Like Hasty, he utilizes a diminuendo after the attack of the d^2 in measure 100 to introduce a change of character from the brillante affectation of the previous phrase, encompassing measures 95 to 99, to a dolce sentiment in the succeeding group, which concludes in measure 105.

As an extension of the same concept, Wright also initiates transitions of character between successive phrases and in larger sections of the formal sections of the first movement. Among other alterations of the temperament of phrases that appear in succession is the change of character between the dolce high *tessitura* material that occurs in bars 116 and 117 and 120 and 121 and the deep, sonorous low-range groupings that succeed each of these two phrases in bars 118 and 119 and 122 and 123. A principal example of a change of mood between larger sections of the formal structure of the movement is Wright's introduction of performance *con fuoco* in measure 69 after the dolce quality of the melodic line throughout the entire statement of the principal theme in measures 57 to 68.

Another manner of acknowledgment of the total formal structure of the Allegro is evidenced in Wright's interpretation of the return of the principal theme. He renders the reappearance of the main theme of the movement more apparent by articulating the g^3 half note in bar 251, which is indicated as tied from the preceding bar in the Breitkopf and Haertel edition. (His employment of articulation in this passage is not followed by the other performers discussed in this book.)

A unique utilization of dynamic phrasing apart from espressivo or emphasized pitches occurs in Wright's performance of measure 148, as is illustrated in example 5.11. In a manner different from that of the other interpreters studied in this text, Wright begins this bar forte, as indicated in the Breitkopf and Haertel edition, and then carries out a diminuendo in the first and second beats to a piano level on the third beat of the same bar.

Example 5.11

According to Wright, volume changes in sequential passages of the Allegro are not interpreted in a terraced fashion. He does note, however, that in reality stepwise gradations of dynamic levels probably do occur in passages of this nature. In his performance the successions of phrases encompassing measures 210 to 214 and 220 to 223 are initiated at the piano level, and a gradual increase in volume is effected to the termination of the passages. In measures 210 and 220 he adds a piano marking to the Breitkopf and Haertel edition.

Other dynamic level alterations of the indications in the Breitkopf and Haertel edition include a somewhat unusual lowering of the volume within the first phrase of the clarinet part, at measure 63, to a piano level. A reduced dynamic level is executed on the repetition of the two-measure phrase in measure 182. Although Wright avoids echolike dynamic contrasts in reiterated phrases of all movements of the concerto, he performs bars 184 and 185 at a slightly quieter level of volume than is utilized for the identical group of pitches in the two previous bars.

Wright prefers a well-defined but varied style of articulation throughout the Allegro. In his interpretation, the tongue is employed specifically to accentuate the rhythmic background, to stress individual pitches, to add force in the melodic line, and to introduce increased variety in the movement.

In accordance with his philosophy that the Allegro must be performed in a lively manner, Wright places considerable emphasis on the use of a distinct style of articulation throughout the movement. It is his opinion that the tongued notes must not be too lengthy, and to this end he frequently makes use of what he terms a "ball-bouncing" style of staccato. He describes this mode of articulation as a dolce effect with increased clarity.

Combined with this approach to articulation is his belief that the durations of tongued pitches in the first movement must be varied. Among the most conspicuous examples of his diversification of articulation styles in the Allegro is the phrase that includes measures 69 to 75. In this passage the sixteenth notes in bar 69 are tongued sharply, in conjunction with a forceful interpretation of the bar as a whole, and the eighth notes in bar 71 are articulated in a legato manner, in accord with Wright's reversion to a more dolce attitude in the latter half of the phrase.

Wright adds articulation in a number of passages in the opening movement to further emphasize the rhythmic pulse. In measures 143 and 144 (example 5.12), and identically in measures 331 to 333, he introduces tonguing on the third and fourth sixteenth notes of every four-note grouping in order to accentuate all beats of the metric pulse. Similarly, he adds articulation on the first sixteenth notes of all beats in bars 337 and 338 to enhance the prominence of the rhythmic pulse.

Example 5.12

In addition to the *tenuto* effects that Wright frequently utilizes to highlight prominent pitches in the solo line of the first movement, he also employs articulations to accentuate specific notes. In a pattern of articulation similar to that of measures 143 and 144, he tongues the third and fourth sixteenth notes on the initial beats of measures 146 and 147 (example 5.5) to stress the lowest pitches of the arpeggios contained therein. For added emphasis, the g^4 on the third beat of bar 147 and the e^4 on the third beat of bar 339 are also tongued.

To increase the impetus of measure 186, Wright tongues the first and third sixteenth notes on the latter two beats of the measure (example 5.13). It is also Wright's belief that the introduction of articulation enhances the variety of the passage, since each of the six preceding measures is slurred in its entirety. Notably, this bar is performed with the same articulations as those observed in the interpretations of Hasty and Gigliotti.

Example 5.13

Notational changes executed by Wright in his interpretation of the Allegro include alterations in individual pitches and in octave positions of extended passages. A somewhat unusual change in notation is preferred but not always performed by Wright on the first beat of measure 73. As seen in example 5.14, he sometimes changes the first note of the measure, the e³, to a g³. Another unique notational change occurs in measures 324 and 325, where both the b¹ and the d¹ on the fourth beats of each measure are changed to g¹ and b¹ (example 5.15). Gigliotti alters the b¹ on the fourth beat of these two bars but not the d¹. As with all the clarinetists discussed in this text thus far, Wright plays the third and fourth beats of measures 146 and 147 an octave higher (example 5.5). Like Hasty, he also performs the first two beats of bar 333 an octave above the pitches indicated in the Breitkopf and Haertel edition.

Example 5.14

Example 5.15

ADAGIO MOVEMENT

In his rendition of the Adagio, Wright places the emphasis on quality and control of tone above all other elements. Other devices that receive special attention in his performance of this movement include the expressiveness of the melodic line, dynamic phrasing, rhythm, ornamentation, articulation, and treatment of the cadenza. It should be noted that Wright does not perform the movement with any notational changes from what is indicated in the Breitkopf and Haertel edition.

As in the Allegro, the primary elements employed by Wright to enhance the expressiveness of the melodic line of the Adagio are the *tenuto* device and dynamic phrasing. Specific illustrations of his utilization of *tenuto* effects in the solo line include the added duration allotted the a^3 in bar 2 and the c^3 in bar 4 (example 5.16), and the *tenuto* that appears on the d^3 that occurs as the second pitch in bars 41 and 90. (Hasty, Marcellus, and Gigliotti also deal in some manner with the expansive leap between the g^1 and d^3 in measures 41 and 90.)

Example 5.16

Passages in which dynamic phrasing is utilized for increased feeling in the solo part include the initial phrase for the instrument in the Adagio movement and each of the phrases in the B section of the formal structure. In the opening statement, the three initial internal groups of pitches in bars 1, 3, and 5 are performed with increasing fervor and dynamic tension. In addition, Wright introduces a crescendo in measure 6, which further increases the dynamic tension of the passage, before a dynamic release on the first beat of the succeeding measure. It is his opinion that the first phrase encompasses measures 1 through 8; however, he considers the melodic material contained in the third beat of measure 7 and the first beat of measure 8 to represent an extension in the formal structure of the passage.

Wright views the middle section of the Adagio, including bars 33 to 59, as a succession of beautiful phrases, each of which should be performed in a different manner. Consequently, he continually varies the dynamic phrasing and character of each subsequent statement in this section. In his rendition the group of pitches in bars 33 and 34 is played very dolce and is then followed by a more forceful statement in bars 35 and 36. This pattern of character change is continued with the next two phrases, which are contained in measures 37 to 40. The first of these two groupings is performed in a tender and dolce fashion, and the second is a stronger statement that leads to succeeding phrases of the section.

Wright essentially observes the dynamic markings for the Adagio as indicated in the Breitkopf and Haertel edition. He does, however, exaggerate certain indications in order to highlight portions of the formal structure of the movement. Like all the other performers discussed in this text, Wright accentuates the return of the principal theme in bar 60 by a volume level that is noticeably quieter than the dynamic level chosen for the initial statement of the material. In measure 60, he employs a volume level that approaches *sotto voce*, while his dynamic level for measure 1 is low, but not pianissimo. Wright performs the reiterations of short phrases in the Adagio at a lower volume level and with a different tone color. Interestingly, the only echo in his rendition of the entire concerto appears in bar 85 of the Adagio. In this passage, which is an exact repetition of the two preceding measures, a slight interruption in the rhythmic pulse and a change in tone color accompany the *subito* piano volume executed in measure 85. Similarly, bar 89, which is an exact repetition of pitches at an octave below the previous bar, is performed more quietly.

Wright employs fluctuations in the tempo of the movement as another device for the enhancement of the expressiveness of the solo line. In his interpretation bars 5 and 6 are performed with a slight increase in the tempo as the phrase proceeds to the release of the dynamic tension in bar 7. Like all of the other performers analyzed in this book, he plays measures 33 to 59 with a freedom in the rhythm.

He also slightly increases the tempo of that section if the initial rate of
the metric pulse chosen for the second movement is slow (Wright
notes that he has performed the Adagio with and without this
quickening of tempo). In a reverse manner, as the tension of the
movement subsides near the end, he plays the last three eighth notes
of measure 96 with a relaxation in the rhythmic pulse. As a result of
this ritardando, the final f^2 in the subsequent bar is performed with
added duration.

As is illustrated in example 5.17, Wright adds slurs to each of the
two groups of thirty-second notes on the second beat of measure 55
(bar 58 is articulated in an identical manner). No other alterations of
articulations occur in his interpretation of the Adagio.

Example 5.17

With regard to the ornamentation of the movement, Wright
performs the grace notes that appear before the third beats in
measures 7, 22, 66, and 74 on the beats, giving them the value of
sixteenth notes. Both Wright and Gigliotti agree in their interpretations of these particular embellishments. Wright believes that the
grace notes in these passages are especially beautiful pitches and must
be allowed sufficient duration to be audible to the listener. Both of the
trills in the Adagio are initiated from the higher pitch in Wright's
interpretation. It should be noted that they are approached from a
higher pitch in the melodic line and are therefore performed in
accordance with the rule for trills of the classical period.

The material that Wright chooses for the cadenza of the second
movement is derived from previous material in the concerto and
from Mozart's Clarinet Quintet. Wright begins the cadenza with
pitches from the opening tutti of the Allegro (example 5.18) and
concludes with the final nine pitches of the quintet cadenza. The
additional notes in Wright's cadenza are similar to those found in the
cadenza that Carl Baerman wrote for his edition of the concerto.

Example 5.18

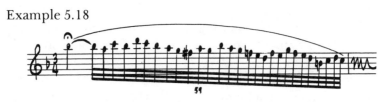

RONDO MOVEMENT

In his overall conception of the Rondo, it is Wright's belief that the movement must be performed in a manner that will render it light in character. While this concept primarily influences his interpretation of the melodic line, it also affects his choice of articulations in the movement, as well as his approach to the solo line, ornamentation, phrasing, fluctuations in the tempo, dynamic phrasing, dynamics, articulation, and notational changes. As in all the other interpretations observed in this text, Wright frequently integrates his utilization of specific devices for increased emphasis of various parameters of the work. In the Rondo he combines fluctuations in the rhythmic pulse with espressivo elements to accentuate changes of character within individual phrases.

As in the previous movements, Wright frequently employs *tenuto* effects in the Rondo to enhance the expressiveness of the solo part and to accentuate features of the harmony. In order to maintain the buoyant nature that he desires for the movement, however, he avoids stretching this device to excessive lengths, which might result in lags in the rhythmic pulse.

Among those pitches upon which Wright employs *tenuto* playing for additional feeling are the c^2 on the first beat of bar 104 (example 5.19) and the three eighth notes in the latter halves of bars 209, 211, and 213. Each of the groups of eighth notes in the latter three measures is performed with increased expressiveness, with measure 213 (example 5.20) receiving the most expressive emphasis. Interestingly, Hasty utilizes a similar amount of expression in his rendition of bar 213.

Example 5.19

Example 5.20

Wright employs *tenuto* effects in measures 61 and 63 to highlight the underlying harmonic background of this passage. In measure 61 he performs the f³ on the first beat, which represents the seventh of the accompaniment sonority, with added duration. The placement of a *tenuto* device on the c² sharp on the first beat of measure 63 is illustrative of his accentuation of nonharmonic tones in the final movement.

Each of the trills in the Rondo is initiated in accordance with the pattern established in the Allegro and Adagio movements. Since the trills in measures 50, 177, and 345 are approached from lower pitches in the solo line, they are begun from the written notes. Conversely, the trilled pitches in bars 96, 315, and 317 are preceded by higher pitches in the melodic line; hence they are initiated from the note above the written pitch.

In his approach to the phrasing of the movement, Wright adheres primarily to the internal grouping of pitches indicated in the Breitkopf and Haertel edition. Of particular note, however, is his concept of character change in successive phrases, as was also observed in his interpretation of the Allegro. Two passages that provide examples of mood change in phrases that follow one another occur in measures 91 to 101 and 319 to 326. The material in bars 99 to 101 is performed dolce, in contrast to the preceding phrase, encompassing bars 91 to 97, which Wright renders in a more forceful manner. Similarly, the phrase *con fuoco* included in measures 319 to 322 is succeeded by a dolce passage that encompasses measures 323 to 325 (example 5.21) to accentuate the more relaxed manner of the latter phrase, which Wright performs slightly below tempo. (This feature is not found in the other interpretations dicussed in this book.) Wright notes that the character change to dolce in bar 323 actually begins with the tutti part in the preceding measure and that the original tempo of the Rondo is resumed in bar 327.

Example 5.21

In addition to the two fermatas indicated by the Breitkopf and Haertel edition in measures 219 and 221 and the tempo change noted above, Wright employs deviations in the metric pulse to stress the overall formal structure and to enhance the light character of the last movement. As in Marcellus's rendition, Wright utilizes a *calando* style of execution in bar 333 to decrease the tempo on the final appearance of the principal theme in bar 334. He retains the slower tempo, combined with a noticeably softer dynamic level, until measure 340, where the original tempo is regained. For a heightened feeling of animation near the close of the movement, Wright performs the final three phrases of the clarinet part, including bars 340 to 346, *stringendo.*

The overall formal structure of the Rondo is also highlighted in certain instances by dynamic phrasing. To signal the beginning of a new structural division in measure 186, Wright performs the preceding measure with a crescendo, rather than the diminuendo that is indicated in the Breitkopf and Haertel edition.

Wright frequently employs a combination of dynamic phrasing and alterations in dynamic levels to introduce variety into successive statements of the principal theme of the Rondo movement. With the exception of the performance of the final statement of the main theme, this feature of his interpretation is not employed in the renditions of Hasty, Marcellus, or Gigliotti. In bar 8 of the initial introduction of the theme, he adds a crescendo to the c^2 on the fourth beat, thus emphasizing the second half of the measure, rather than making a crescendo in bar 7 to stress the c^2 on the first half of the bar, as Hasty does. On the second appearance of the main theme Wright plays the fourth through sixth beats of measure 30 piano (example 5.22). In a later statement of the theme, measure 276 is performed identically. Contrary to the preceding statement of the theme, which ends piano, he performs measure 120 forte, with a crescendo to the c^2 in the subsequent bar. According to Wright, one reason for the rendition of this bar at the forte level is to align the solo part with the tutti material that begins in the succeeding measure. Wright performs the final statement of the main theme at a quiet dynamic level.

Example 5.22

Another interesting facet of Wright's approach to the dynamics of the Rondo movement is his interpretation of the sequential passage that includes measures 105 to 110 (and measures 238 to 243). As illustrated in example 5.23, Wright interprets the three dynamic levels indicated in the Breitkopf and Haertel edition in a reverse fashion. In his rendition of the passage, the mezzo forte marking in bar 105 is changed to pianissimo, the piano in bar 107 remains unaltered, and the pianissimo level in bar 109 is changed to mezzo forte.

Example 5.23

It is of note that Wright increases the volume level indicated in measure 84 of the Breitkopf and Haertel edition but does not lower the dynamics on the reiteration of the phrase. He replaces the piano indication in this bar with a forte marking, but, in accordance with his philosophy on repeated phrases, he does not lower the dynamic level in bar 86 to create an echo effect.

According to Wright, the style of the articulated sixteenth notes of the Rondo remains the same as that of tongued sixteenth notes in the Allegro. He does not attempt to tongue the sixteenth notes in the

Rondo to make them shorter; however, since the movement is in six/eight meter, performed two beats per measure, there are six sixteenth notes per beat; hence they are shorter than the sixteenth notes of the Allegro. Wright also notes that he does articulate more frequently in sixteenth-note passages in the Rondo than in the first two movements of the work. It should be added that in his rendition of the Rondo he adheres more closely to the articulations indicated in the Breitkopf and Haertel edition than he does to those in the Allegro movement.

In a number of passages in the movement Wright adds articulations to enhance the character of the work. Interestingly, unlike the other clarinetists dealt with in this book, he tongues the third and sixth eighth notes of measures 59 (example 5.24) and 190. In the interest of conformity and balance, he articulates the pitches on the fifth and sixth beats of bar 163 in a similar manner. He adds a slur between the fourth and fifth beats of bar 171 to create a similar pattern of articulation. He believes that this arrangement of tongued pitches adds a feeling of lightness to the passages. To further intensify the spirit of the movement, Wright articulates all sixteenth and eighth notes in measures 91 and 92 (example 5.25) and also tongues on the first and fourth beats of measures 208 to 213 rather than slurring the measure as indicated in the Breitkopf and Haertel edition (example 5.26). Finally, for added interest and increased force in the melodic line, he articulates the f^3 sharp on the fourth beat of bar 93. Interestingly, both Hasty and Gigliotti articulate measures 93 and 94 in the same manner, but for different reasons.

Example 5.24

Example 5.25

Example 5.26

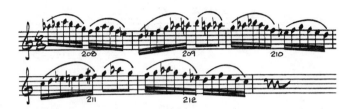

Slurs are added in a number of passages in Wright's interpretation of the Rondo movement to improve the continuity between the solo and tutti parts and to build a greater continuum of sound. Wright slurs the sixteenth notes in the latter halves of bars 30 and 276 to match the articulations of the clarinet part with the tutti sections that begin in bars 31 and 277. Passages in which groups of six sixteenth notes on the first three beats of the measure are slurred occur in measures 61 and 62 (example 5.27), and identically in measures 192 and 193, and measures 88 and 89, including the e^4 on the fourth beat (example 5.28). The sixteenth notes on the fourth through sixth beats of measures 302 to 306 are slurred as they are by Marcellus and Gigliotti. Wright also slurs sixteenth notes in two groupings of six in bars 69 (example 5.29), 86 (example 5.30), 311 to 313 (example 5.31), and 342 (example 5.32). He slurs measures 84 (example 5.30) and 120 each in its entirety.

Example 5.27

Example 5.28

Example 5.29

Example 5.30

Example 5.31

Example 5.32

In addition to changes in articulations indicated in the Breitkopf and Haertel edition, Wright alters several pitches in the Rondo. Like all the other performers discussed thus far, Wright changes the a^1 appearing on the fifth beat of bar 169 to a b^1 flat so that the affected group of pitches will conform to the pattern of intervals appearing later in the sequence in bars 171 and 173. Like Hasty, he adds a grace note b^1 flat before the eighth note on the fifth beat of measure 205. Finally, like Gigliotti, Wright plays the passage extending from the fourth beat of measure 311 through the third beat of measure 313 an octave lower than it is written in the Breitkopf and Haertel edition, with the exception of the c^1 on the second beats of measures 312 and 313, which is performed as an f^1. According to Wright, the transposition of these three bars down an octave allows the passage to conform more closely to the alleged original basset clarinet version of the phrase.

SIX

Rudolf Jettel's Interpretation

Rudolf Jettel was born in Vienna, Austria, and has lived and worked there all of his life. He received his musical training at the Vienna Academy. His teacher was Victor Polatschek, who later emigrated to the United States and held the solo clarinet position in the Boston Symphony Orchestra. Jettel's primary orchestral experience was performance with the Vienna Philharmonic, where he was principal clarinetist for thirty-six years, and also with the Hofburg Kapelle Orchestra, a position he held for twenty-five years. He recorded the Mozart Clarinet Concerto with the Vienna Symphony Orchestra in 1952. Since his retirement from orchestral performance, Jettel has retained his position as professor of clarinet at the Vienna Academy, where he teaches a large class. As do all of Vienna's clarinetists, he plays an Oehler system clarinet, which is also called the German clarinet.

This artist-teacher's interpretation of the concerto is the combined result of both a lifetime spent in a city rich in the tradition of Mozart's performance and information about the concerto that was given to him by his teacher. According to Jettel, Polatschek possessed a hand-written copy of the concerto that possibly originally belonged to one of Anton Stadler's students. In his teaching of the work Polatschek frequently alluded to remarks about the concerto that were attributed to both Stadler and Mozart.

Jettel's approach to the entire concerto is characterized by a singing, somewhat free approach to the melodic line. Though he cautions against excessive *rubato* and tempo fluctuation that might dissipate the work's classical characteristics, he frequently utilizes both *tenuto* playing and *rubato* in his interpretation of the work.

In addition to the use throughout the entire concerto of *tenuto* effects for expressive purposes, he calls for added length for the beginning notes of nearly all arpeggios and runs in the Allegro and Rondo movements. These *tenuto* effects, often followed by a slight quickening of the tempo, lend both improvisatory and bravura qualities to the passages in which they are used.

In the first and last movements he also introduces slight tempo fluctuations more often than do his European counterparts. The *rubato* passages that stand out in Jettel's interpretation take the form of accelerandos followed by poco ritardandos, or of isolated quickenings and slowings of phrase groups.

Ornamentations—that is, trills—in the concerto are always negotiated from the written note in Jettel's interpretation. This represents a departure both from the standard approach to ornamentation in the classical era and from the practice of most American clarinetists (for example, Hasty, Marcellus, Gigliotti, or Wright). The American players perform most of the trills in the work in an inverted fashion, with a *tenuto* performance of the beginning note.

In his approach to the larger formal aspects of the concerto, Jettel feels that the reprises should always be slightly different from the initial statements of the main themes. In the Allegro and Adagio movements he consequently highlights the return of the principal themes by changing the dynamic levels. In both movements the repeats of recurring themes are played at softer dynamic levels than are the initial statements. Jettel also calls the listener's attention to repeated and sequential phrases throughout the work in a similar manner. Reiterated and successive passages are always executed at a different dynamic level than the original statements.

Jettel's treatment of articulation in the concerto also represents a deviation from the styles of the American performers discussed in this book. With regard to articulation of the sixteenth note passages, Jettel calls for a great deal more articulation than do the Americans. (Interestingly, his views on articulation in the work are quite similar to the other European clarinetists included in this text.) In each of the three movements Jettel adheres quite closely to the articulation indicated in the Breitkopf and Haertel edition, the edition that he prefers. It must be added that he proposes a style of articulation for the concerto that is not too *secco.* The rapid tongued passages are consequently more lucid than they might be if slurred, but are not interrupted to the point that their melodic momentum is lost.

Jettel adheres strictly to the notation of the printed Breitkopf and Haertel edition of the concerto. He makes no changes other than one deletion in the Allegro and two corrections for printer's errors or omissions in the Rondo movement. Interestingly, Jettel makes no octave transpositions in deference to the alleged autograph manuscript for basset clarinet.

ALLEGRO MOVEMENT

In his interpretation of the melodic line of the Allegro movement, Jettel adheres to a philosophy of "singing through the clarinet." He makes frequent use of *tenuto* devices both to increase expressiveness and to begin many arpeggiated figures. His use of *tenuto* effects for espressivo in measures 80 (example 6.1), 97, and 110 (example 6.2) is unique among the performances addressed thus far in this book. Passages in which *tenuto* effects are added on the first sixteenth notes of arpeggiated figures include bars 83 (example 6.3), 108, 109, 138, 139, 181, and 183.

Example 6.1

Example 6.2

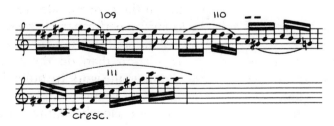

Example 6.3

Fluctuations in tempo or *rubati* constitute the most unusual aspect of Jettel's interpretation of the melodic line of the Allegro. While he employs slight ritardandos in many instances throughout the Allegro, his inclusion of this device on the third and fourth beats of bar 124 (example 6.4) is unusual. Passages where he has uniquely combined both accelerandos and ritardandos include bars 82 to 84 (example 6.3), 123 and 124 (example 6.4), and 150 to 152 (example 6.5), where the accelerando and ritardando are reversed.

Example 6.4

Example 6.5

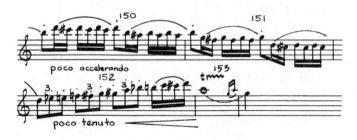

In contrast to his frequent employment of *rubato* in the first movement, Jettel performs the sixteenth notes in bars 134 to 140 (example 6.6) in strict tempo. In his words they should be executed in a very "authoritative" manner.

Example 6.6

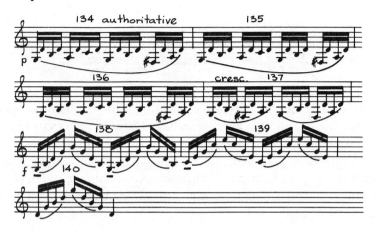

The formal structure of the Allegro movement is frequently illuminated through dynamic contrast and dynamic phrasing. Repeated phrases, such as those encountered in measures 172 to 176 and 180 to 182, are performed at the forte level on the initial statement and at a piano level on the restatement. Sequential phrases like those found in measures 87 to 91 are treated with terraced dynamic levels from piano and mezzo piano to forte. Jettel couples dynamics with dynamic phrasing in a unique manner in the sequential phrase group contained in measures 145 to 147 (example 6.7), in which he begins each of the three phrases in the sequence at the forte level and effects a diminuendo as each arpeggio ascends. Jettel highlights the return of the principal theme of the Allegro in a different and unique manner. He changes the dynamic marking of the first statement of the theme (bar 57) from piano to mezzo forte. He later drops in a diminuendo to a piano level on the fourth beat of bar 248 thus calling greater attention to the soft restatement of the melodic material (example 6.8).

Example 6.7

Example 6.8

Another unique and interesting combination of dynamic change and dynamic phrasing is utilized in bars 190 and 191 (example 6.9). In measure 190 the dynamic marking on the second beat is changed from forte to piano, thus changing the character of the consequent portion of the phrase from bravura to dolce. The harmonic change between bars 190 and 191 is also emphasized through the use of dynamic phrasing.

Example 6.9

With the exception of a few passages where slurs are added, Jettel adheres to the articulations indicated in the Breitkopf and Haertel edition. Measures with added slurs, which contain either sixteenth note runs or arpeggios, are so few that all can be noted. Jettel adds slurs to the phrase groups contained in bar 142, as do all the American clarinetists mentioned in this text, and in measures 145 to 147 (example 6.7), 183, in which the first and second and eighth and ninth sixteenth notes are slurred, and 338.

Jettel makes no notational changes in the Allegro movement. Unlike Hasty, Marcellus, Gigliotti, or Wright, however, he deletes all of measure 333 (example 6.10). He defends this decision on the grounds that it is an excess bar, pointing out that it is not found in the exposition of the movement. The absence of the availability of a downward transposition of the passage as is allegedly contained in the autograph manuscript of the concerto and the resultant static repetition may also influence his decision to remove the measure.

Example 6.10

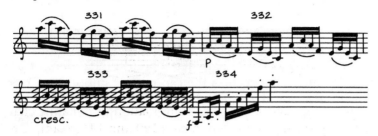

ADAGIO MOVEMENT

According to Jettel, the Adagio movement must be performed in a highly expressive manner; in his words, "always from the heart." In light of that statement, he introduces surprisingly few *tenuto* effects or other expressive devices in this section of the concerto.

Unique features of his interpretation of the melodic line include his treatment of the finish notes of the trill in bar 92 (example 6.11). Jettel performs the finish notes in measure 92 more slowly than the trilled notes that preceded them. Concurrently he employs a diminuendo throughout the measure to a piano dynamic level on the first beat of measure 93. Another interesting factor of Jettel's interpretation is his treatment of the final note of the movement, the f^2 in measure 98. This note is executed in a "blank" fashion, absent of tonal color, and is held longer than the indicated half note duration.

Example 6.11

Other than the *rubato* utilized in measure 92, Jettel does not employ other tempo changes or *rubati* in his attempt to add expressiveness to the melodic line of the Adagio. Unlike most other modern performers of the concerto, he even performs the B section of the second movement without tempo change.

Jettel's only deviation from the indicated articulation of the Adagio movement is made in measure 91 (example 6.11). Here he slurs all sixteenth-note triplets and tongues the last four sixteenth notes in a legato style.

For the cadenza in the Adagio, Jettel prefers the cadenza from the Clarinet Quintet. He executes the cadenza as smoothly as possible and avoids making the internal phrase groupings of the passage overly apparent. He believes that the performer should breathe at the end of the cadenza.

RONDO

Jettel's use of *rubato* in the melodic line of the Rondo is similar to his employment of the device in the Allegro movement of the concerto. Accelerandos and *rallentandos* are used both singularly and in combination, and *tenuto* markings are frequently placed over the beginning sixteenth notes of arpeggiated figures and runs.

Of note are the passages included in measure 49 (example 6.12), in which the fourth through sixth beats are performed poco *più mosso;* in bar 310 (example 6.13), where a poco *tenuto* effect is added on the sixteenth notes of the last three beats; in measures 311 to 313 (example 6.13), which are performed poco *più mosso* because of the technical difficulty caused by frequent rapid crossing of the register change on the clarinet; and in measures 175 and 176 (example 6.14), where both accelerando and *rallentando* are added.

Example 6.12

Example 6.13

Example 6.14

Perhaps Jettel's most unique application of *rubato* in the final movement may be found in measures 1 and 2 (example 6.15). The first statement of the Rondo theme is performed as an introductory phrase, that is, with the first two sixteenth notes handled in a broader fashion and at a slower tempo than those of the remaining portion of the movement. The actual tempo of the movement is assumed at the beginning of bar 2. (The metronome marking that Jettel prefers is approximately eighty-eight beats per minute.)

Example 6.15

As in the preceding movements, Jettel in some instances alters printed dynamic levels in the Rondo to emphasize the character change that occurs between assorted related phrases and to allow the solo part to match the volume level of preceding tutti sections in a better way.

His addition of a mezzo forte dynamic marking in measure 183 (example 6.16), coupled with markedly increased volume and dynamic phrasing in bars 184 and 185, creates a character difference that is not utilized by any other performer discussed in this book. Through this alteration Jettel further augments the many character changes occurring in the Breitkopf and Haertel edition where preceding high *tessitura* passages are marked piano and alternating low-register phrases are indicated as forte.

The volume levels of two passages in the Rondo movement are raised so that the entry of the solo line will be more dynamically compatible with the preceding tutti part. Bar 57 (example 6.17) is raised from piano to poco piano, and measure 301 is changed from piano to the mezzo forte level.

Example 6.16

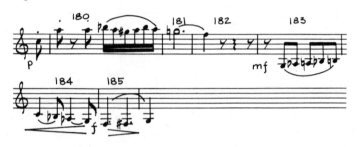

Example 6.17

As in previous movements, Jettel closely adheres to the articulations of the Breitkopf and Haertel edition in the Rondo. His alterations of articulation are so few in the final movement that all can be noted. Articulations are added in measure 6 (example 6.18) and in all subsequent appearances of the same material, and on the third and sixth eighth notes of measure 59 (example 6.17). Deleted articulations are found in bar 7 (example 6.18), where Jettel adds slurs to the sixteenth notes on the first and fourth beats (as he does on all recurrences of the Rondo theme); in measures 20 and 21 (and all subsequent appearances of the phrase), in which he slurs the first three sixteenth notes, as opposed to only the first two; and in the entire passage contained in measures 311 to 313 (example 6.13).

Example 6.18

SEVEN

Ulysse Delécluse's Interpretation

Ulysse Delécluse lives in Paris, France. He received his musical training at the Paris Conservatoire under the tutelage of Auguste Perier, whom Delécluse later succeeded as professor of clarinet. During his musical career Delécluse has won acclaim as a teacher, as an orchestral performer, and as a soloist on his instrument.

Delécluse bases his interpretative decisions in the concerto upon both the musical training that he received from Perier and his own musical taste. He has performed the work on many occasions under the batons of such conductors as Lorin Maazel, Hans Rosbaud, and Carl Baumgartner. Delécluse's involvement with the concerto has also led to his own edition of the work, which was published by Leduc in 1951.

While Delécluse's overall conception of the concerto is melodic, he frequently leans toward a more classical stylistic approach. He makes limited use of *rubato* and tempo fluctuations for expressive purposes and relies heavily on dynamic devices as a means of maintaining and increasing musical interest in the work.

He frequently utilizes sudden and unprepared dynamic changes in the concerto, with resulting surprises for the listener. Interestingly, many such volume changes occur in all of the three movements within single phrases and result in subtle character changes similar to those developed in Marcellus's interpretation of the concerto.

As Delécluse remarks, the French interpretation of the concerto is lighter than the approach to the work assumed by performers of other nationalities. His handling of both dynamics and articulation in the work adds credence to that statement. Many of the dynamic alterations made by the artist-teacher Delécluse involve an interesting lowering of the volume levels printed in the Breitkopf and Haertel edition of the work. Perusal of Delécluse's own edition of the concerto also reveals a propensity for softer dynamic levels.

Delécluse's frequent use of articulation in the concerto reinforces his effort to lend a light, buoyant feeling to the work. He follows nearly all of the articulations indicated in the Breitkopf and Haertel edition.

Like Jettel, Delécluse executes all trills in the concerto from the written note. This is somewhat unexpected in view of his tendency toward a classical interpretation.

As most of the other clarinetists discussed in this book do, Delécluse performs the returns of the larger sections of the work in the same manner as the initial statements. However, he frequently illuminates portions of interior phrases by using dynamic changes. Repeated phrases and sequential passages in his performance are interestingly afforded slightly less attention than they are in other performances studied in this text.

With one exception, Delécluse alters only those pitches in the concerto that appear to be printer's errors. He does not transpose any passages in the work in recognition of the alleged basset clarinet version.

ALLEGRO MOVEMENT

Delécluse performs the solo line of the Allegro essentially as it is dictated in the printed score. He adds only a small number of espressivo devices and avoids additional *rubati* or tempo fluctuations. He prefers a tempo marking of 120 to 126 beats per minute for the Allegro.

Espressivo devices of note include *tenuto* effects and accents that highlight pitches not usually stressed in performance of the concerto. Increased breadth and weight in the line are obtained through use of *tenuto* playing on the fourth beat of bar 93 (example 7.1) and on the first two sixteenth notes of bar 199 (example 7.2). Also unique is Delécluse's use of accents on the whole note in bar 187 and the attacks of the trilled half notes in measures 225 and 226.

Example 7.1

Example 7.2

In the Allegro movement Delécluse makes some use of dynamics to illuminate reiterated and sequential phrases and, most significantly, to call attention to the internal construction of selected single phrases. His treatment of repeated and sequential phrases in this movement takes the form of contrasted and terraced dynamics, effects that many other clarinetists employ. Of special note is his use of contrasted dynamics to emphasize the two parts of the phrase contained in measures 198 and 199 (example 7.2). In this passage Delécluse performs the antecedent or "question" portion of the phrase piano, without a crescendo. He then executes the consequent answering part of the phrase at the forte level, thus allowing him to produce a marked contrast in the respective musical statements. This overall effect is carried out without involving the *rubato* stylisms or tempo changes that are often utilized in this passage.

As in the entire concerto, Delécluse closely adheres to articulations in the Allegro as they appear in the Breitkopf and Haertel edition. The large number of tongued passages that result stem from his philosophy that the performer's interpretation of a work is colored by his use of articulation. In the Allegro movement, Delécluse's only changes in the printed articulation occur in the form of slurs, which he adds to the first two sixteenth notes on beats one and three of measure 83, and in bar 142, where he slurs all of the sixteenth notes.

Delécluse makes an unusual notational change in bar 280 of the Allegro (example 7.3). Unlike all of the other clarinetists analyzed in this text, he changes the a¹ on the second eighth note of the measure to a¹ flat.

Example 7.3

ADAGIO MOVEMENT

Delécluse presents the Adagio movement in a calm, *cantabile* manner. For increased expressiveness in selected passages of the movement he also employs additional espressivo, *tenuto* playing, dynamic phrasing, *rubato,* and notational alteration.

Delécluse uses espressivo and *tenuto* combinations in bar 6 on the final three eighth notes and in bar 82 on the first *appoggiatura* before the third beat. These *tenuto* effects are not unique to Delécluse's performance; they exemplify a nearly universal mode of interpretation given to many passages of the concerto.

Delécluse's employment of dynamic phrasing for increased expressiveness is especially imaginative and unique in two passages. His inclusion of both a crescendo and diminuendo on the first quarter note of bar 1 and a quiet dynamic level on the subsequent f³ establishes a calm, profound mood for the Adagio (example 7.4). His use of a crescendo on the three successive quarter notes in bar 97 (example 7.5), coupled with an alteration of the printed pianissimo level to mezzo forte volume, allows the final f in measure 98 to serve as a confirmation of the preceding musical statements.

Example 7.4

Example 7.5

Delécluse uses *rubato* in three passages in the Adagio in order to establish, through rhythmic fluctuation, both an expressive feel and a rhapsodic temperament. In bar 35 (example 7.6) his *rubato* is in the form of a *tenuto* effect on the first thirty-second note of the measure. *Rubati* encompass entire measures in bars 55 (example 7.7) and 57. In each of these two bars the first group of thirty-second notes is executed more slowly than the prevailing tempo, and the subsequent grouping, on the third beat, is performed with an accelerando to regain the initial speed of the rhythmic pulse.

Example 7.6

Example 7.7

Of particular note is the unique interpretation that Delécluse lends to the rhythmic figure occurring on the third beat of bar 93 (example 7.8). Unlike all of the other clarinetists discussed in this book, he performs the five sixteenth notes as a quintuplet rather than as a duplet-triplet combination, as it is indicated in the Breitkopf and Haertel edition. The resulting effect is a less accented, more flowing beginning for the phrase that is initiated by the figure.

Example 7.8

Delécluse's treatment of the larger structural aspects of the Adagio is not unique to his interpretation. This is interesting, however, in light of the fact that he avoids additional tempo changes in the Allegro.

Like many other clarinetists, he performs the middle (B) section at a slightly faster tempo than the rest of the movement, returning to the initial tempo after the cadenza on the restatement of the principal theme.

With regard to phrase structure in the second movement, Delécluse emphasizes both reiterated passages and the differences between internal portions of certain phrases. It is noteworthy that he does not perform the two sequential passages in the Adagio with terraced dynamics. Delécluse does illuminate repeated phrases through dynamic contrast, as do other performers. Volume changes that contrast portions of phrases may be found in measures 21 to 24, where the consequent part of the phrase in bar 23 is marked piano; in bars 35 and 36 (see example 7.6), with the antecedent portion of the passage changed to forte and the consequent part contrasted at the piano level; and in measures 41 to 44 (example 7.9), in which the phrase begins forte and drops in a diminuendo to a piano level to highlight the consequent portion.

Example 7.9

Delécluse prefers to use the quintet cadenza for the cadenza of the Adagio. In his view that cadenza serves as a bridge to connect the middle section of the movement to the return of the principal theme. He therefore performs the final four pitches of the passage in the tempo of the movement and proceeds to the principal theme in bar 60 without pausing either to phrase or to breathe.

RONDO

Delécluse performs the melodic line of the Rondo with very few added espressivo, legato, and *rubato* effects. His only noteworthy additions of espressivo and legato occur in bar 4 (example 7.10) and in all similar recurrences of this theme. Delécluse's use of the espressivo device in these passages is similar to that of a number of American interpreters.

Example 7.10

Delécluse prefers a metronome marking of eighty-eight beats per minute for the Rondo, deviating from this tempo in only two measures. Like all of the other artists cited in this text, he performs measures 220 and 221 slightly below tempo and regains the initial tempo in bar 222.

Delécluse highlights the final return of the Rondo theme by increasing the volume. He performs the final section, beginning in measure 334, mezzo forte rather than the piano level indicated in the Breitkopf and Haertel edition.

As in the two preceding movements, Delécluse frequently illuminates both the phrase structure and the internal components of phrases by employing dynamic contrast. His use of volume changes within the internal phrase structure of the third movement often constitutes the unique feature of his interpretation.

Unlike all the other performers discussed in this book, Delécluse highlights the repeated phrases that begin in measures 301, 303, and 305 (example 7.11) through terraced dynamics. He executes the initial statement of the phrase piano, as it is indicated in the Breitkopf and Haertel edition, and raises the two subsequent passages to mezzo forte and forte levels respectively.

Example 7.11

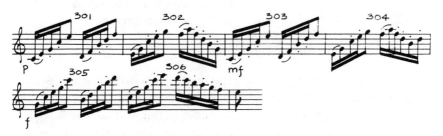

It should be noted that Delécluse does not perform the repeated phrases in bars 84 to 87 and 226 to 230 with contrasting dynamics. In each of these passages he plays both the initial and the reiterated phrases at identical volume levels.

Delécluse utilizes contrasting dynamics to elucidate phrase groupings in three unique passages of the Rondo. An interesting character change occurs within the phrase beginning in bar 36 (example 7.12) as a result of Delécluse's performance of the consequent half, which commences in measure 38, at the pianissimo level. The consequent portions of the phrases beginning in bars 161 (example 7.13), 165, and 205 (example 7.14) are also performed piano, in contrast to their forte beginning sections. Interestingly, these three passages incorporate antecedent sections that contain mostly *chalumeau* pitches and consequent portions with *tessituras* above the staff.

Example 7.12

Example 7.13

Example 7.14

Delécluse deviates from the printed articulations of the Rondo movement in three passages. He adds articulations in bar 59 on the third and sixth eighth notes. Conversely, he adds slurs on the figure in the first half of bar 202 and in measures 311 to 313 (example 7.15), where the sixteenth notes are slurred in groups of two.

Example 7.15

EIGHT

Jack Brymer's
Interpretation

Jack Brymer has pursued much of his career as a professional clarinetist in London, England. In addition to the clarinet instruction that he received from his father, Brymer credits his knowledge of the instrument to his personal observations of music and to his study of such fine English clarinetists as Haydn P. Draper and Frederick Thurston. Brymer's career as an orchestral performer includes sixteen years as principal clarinetist of the Royal Philharmonic Orchestra, nine years as principal clarinetist of the British Broadcasting Orchestra, and from 1972 to the present, as principal clarinetist of the London Symphony Orchestra. Brymer has served as professor of clarinet at the Royal Academy of Music and the Royal Military School of Music, Kneller Hall.

This artist-teacher has performed the concerto many times. Conductors with whom he has played the work include Karl Bohm, Otto Joachim, Otto Klemperer, Pierre Monteux, Sir Malcolm Sargent, Rudolf Kempe, Neville Marriner, and Sir Thomas Beecham. He has recorded the concerto with three different orchestras. He first recorded the work in 1956 with the Royal Philharmonic Orchestra, under Beecham's baton. His subsequent recordings of the concerto have been with the London Symphony, under the direction of Colin Davis, and with the Academy of St.-Martin-in-the-Fields, with Marriner conducting.

Brymer's interpretation of Mozart's Clarinet Concerto is primarily a product of his own musical thinking, although he credits Thomas Beecham with influencing his approach to certain passages in the

151

concerto. Brymer states that the clarinet concerto means more to him personally than any other work written for the clarinet.

In his overall approach to the solo line of the concerto, Brymer utilizes little *rubato* or tempo fluctuation in the Allegro and Adagio movements. Conversely, in the Rondo movement, he makes more frequent use of *rubato* devices.

In a manner different from that of most other European interpreters of the concerto, Brymer utilizes both inverted and noninverted trills. In the Allegro and Rondo, pitches that are trilled from the note above are always preceded by lower pitches in the melodic line.

One of the most interesting features of Brymer's approach to the concerto is his variation in certain passages of tonal focus in conjunction with contrasting *tessituras* in the melodic line, as well as contrasted dynamic levels. Brymer frequently alters the breadth of his tone according to the register of pitches and the prescribed volume level of a passage. Brymer often performs mezzo forte or forte passages in the *chalumeau* register with a broad tone, in the manner of a baritone voice. In contrast, he executes subsequent piano level, high *tessitura* phrases with a thinner tone, with the quality of a high female voice.

In Brymer's rendition of the work most of the alterations of printed dynamic markings are made to illuminate the phrase construction. He frequently utilizes contrasting dynamics in repeated and sequential phrases, as well as in half phrases. Most of the changes that Brymer makes to the printed Breitkopf and Haertel edition constitute a lowering of the existing dynamic level. The result of his volume changes is a light, *semplice* rendition of the concerto.

It is Brymer's philosophy that in addition to the inherent stylistic characteristics of the work, the length of staccato notes in the concerto must be determined according to both the acoustics of the hall in which the work is to be performed and the size of the accompanying orchestra. To enhance the translucent lines in both the solo and the orchestral parts of the work, great care must be used in decisions regarding spacing between pitches. According to Brymer, when performing the work the soloist must compensate for an overly absorbent room by adding length to the tongued notes. Conversely, when performing the concerto in a reverberant concert hall, the soloist must shorten the articulated pitches and utilize the natural echo of the room.

The size of the *ripieno* orchestra must also be considered when determining the length of both tongued and bowed notes in the work. In light of the acoustic considerations and the added reverberation resulting from louder sounds, the length of time between tongued or bowed pitches must be increased or decreased corresponding to the size of the accompanying orchestra.

In terms of frequency of articulation in the concerto, Brymer's interpretation represents a median between the American and European clarinetists analyzed in this text. He slurs many of the extended sixteenth note runs and arpeggios that are marked for articulation in the Breitkopf and Haertel edition.

Brymer frequently alludes to the alleged basset clarinet version of the concerto in his interpretation of the work. He makes octave transpositions in many passages of the Allegro and Rondo movements. He also alters the pitches in the Breitkopf and Haertel edition that are generally accepted as printer's errors.

ALLEGRO MOVEMENT

Brymer's interpretation of the melodic line of the Allegro movement is characterized by a leisurely singing approach. He sets the tempo for the first movement by the speed and feeling of the sixteenth notes in bars 108 and 109 (example 8.1). The pitches in these two measures must have motion and also maintain a *cantabile* quality. Brymer does not utilize any tempo fluctuations or *rubati* other than the fermatas.

Example 8.1

In his treatment of the solo line of the Allegro, Brymer limits his use of added espressivo devices to a small number of added accents and unusual *allentando* (underplaying) effects. He does not call upon *tenuto* playing for enhanced expression in his interpretation of the first movement.

Brymer utilizes supplemental accents in two passages of the Allegro. His addition of accents in measure 188 (example 8.2) provides increased stress on the three descending syncopated quarter notes in that measure. Accents that he introduces on the third beat of measures 210 and 211 reinforce the pulse after a break caused by the sixteenth note rests on the second beats.

Example 8.2

One of the most interesting features of Brymer's rendition of the concerto is his use of an *allentando* effect in two passages of the Allegro movement. He produces an unusual mood with this device, coupling a lowered dynamic range with a calculated absence of dynamic phrasing. The result is a static, unmoving effect in measures 61 and 62 (example 8.3) and in bars 78 to 80 (example 8.4).

Example 8.3

Example 8.4

Unlike the European clarinetists Jettel or Delécluse, Brymer varies his negotiation of trills in the Allegro movement. In his rendition the trilled d² in bar 74 is executed in an inverted fashion, but the remaining trills are performed from the written note. Interestingly, Brymer performs the half-note trills in measure 225 with added finish notes, which create turns in the melodic line as it ascends to the trilled whole note a³ in measure 226.

In addition to employing dynamic change for the previously noted *allentando* effects, Brymer also uses dynamic contrast to highlight the internal formal structure of the Allegro. In his interpretation he illuminates reiterated and sequential phrases as well as internal pitch groupings and contrasting *tessituras* within phrases.

Brymer calls attention to the repeated phrases in bars 172 to 176 and 180 to 182, and uniquely emphasizes the reiterated Alberti material in measures 134 and 135 (example 8.5). In the latter passage the dynamic level of the first of the two measures is raised to mezzo forte, and the volume level of the subsequent bar is lowered to piano.

Example 8.5

Like many other clarinetists, Brymer performs the sequential phrases in bars 184 to 186 with terraced dynamics. His treatment of the sequential passage in bars 220 to 222 (example 8.6) is both singular and noteworthy. Brymer performs the first arpeggiated statement mezzo forte, the second segment forte, and the final ascending arpeggio fortissimo.

Example 8.6

The internal phrase groupings that Brymer chooses to highlight through dynamic contrast are frequently portions of passages that contain pitches of contrasting range. Examples of such passages include measures 69 to 75 (example 8.7), where the descending arpeggio crescendoes to a forte f^1 followed by a piano b^3 on the subsequent portion of the phrase; bars 91 and 92 (example 8.8), in which the consequent secton of the phrase (beginning on a b^3 flat) is lowered dynamically to a piano level; and the beginning of the phrase in bar 94 (example 8.8), commencing at a contrastingly low pitch level, which Brymer raises to a louder volume level. One notable exception to passages coupling dynamically contrasting *tessituras* may be found in the final segment of the sequence begun in measure 184. Brymer chooses a piano dynamic level for the d^3, which is the highest pitch and the final note of the intervallic pattern (example 8.2).

Example 8.7

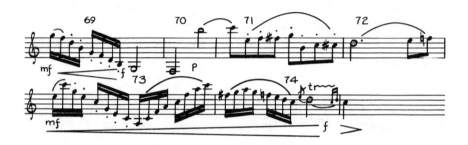

Example 8.8

Brymer's interpretation of the Allegro movement calls for additional dynamic phrasing both to reinforce harmonic progressions and to enhance the contour of the solo line of the movement. He gives greater emphasis to the chordal progressions in measures 65 to 68 (example 8.9) through a crescendo that encompasses the entire phrase to the c^2 in bar 68. Brymer crescendoes to the third beats of both measures 101 and 102 (he professes that Thomas Beecham called his attention to the need for dynamic phrasing in these two measures). The repeated quarter notes in measures 194 and 196 are also given crescendos. Brymer introduces dynamic phrasing in conjunction with the contour of the melodic line in measures 339 to 341 (example 8.10). His performance of dynamics in this passage creates an expansive attitude for this phrase, which closes the movement.

Example 8.9

Example 8.10

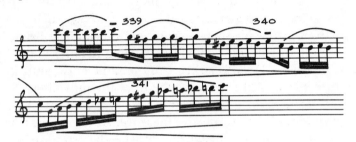

In his approach to the articulation of the Allegro, Brymer adheres closely to the Breitkopf and Haertel edition. His alterations of the published markings include slurs on a small number of sixteenth-note arpeggios and runs and additional tonguing in two passages of the movement.

Brymer adds slurs entirely across each of the sixteenth-note arpeggios in measures 145 to 147 and 334 to 336, and across the two final sixteenth notes and the eighth note in measure 338. He adds articulation in bar 83 (example 8.11) to the third and fourth sixteenth notes on beats three and four. He also tongues the sixteenth notes on the third and fourth beats in measure 186 to separate them into two groups.

Example 8.11

Brymer transposes the second and third beats of measures 146 and 147 of the Allegro an octave higher in deference to the alleged basset clarinet version of the concerto. He prefers either to treat measure 333 as an excess bar and omit it, or to perform it as written, as a basset clarinet measure.

ADAGIO MOVEMENT

Brymer believes that the Adagio movement has special significance among Mozart's concerti in view of the fact that Mozart assigned adagio indications to the slow movements of only three of his works in this genre. In addition, his interpretation of this movement is influenced by his belief that it must be performed in a *semplice* fashion. In accord with this interpretive philosophy, Brymer performs the solo line of the Adagio in a singing manner and adds few expressive devices. He also adheres to the same basic philosophy in his interpretations of the ornamentation of the movement.

Brymer executes the grace notes in bars 7, 23, 66, and 68 directly on the third beat of each respective measure. He allows the ornamentation a short duration in order to maintain the established *semplice* character of the movement. For similar reasons the finish notes for the trill in measure 92 are elongated and performed softly.

Interestingly, Brymer determines the tempo for the Adagio according to the size of the accompanying orchestra. In his view, the larger the ensemble, the slower the tempo one can choose, because of the increased sustaining power of a greater number of instrumentalists.

With only one exception, Brymer does not vary the tempo of the Adagio. According to Brymer the B section of the Adagio should be dramatic but not declamatory, and consequently should not be emphasized by tempo changes. The only fluctuation in his established tempo for the movement therefore occurs in bar 93, where he performs the quintuplet on the third beat in a leisurely manner as a duplet-triplet figure.

Brymer utilizes contrasting volume levels in the second movement to elucidate both the overall phrase structure and internal phrase groupings. As most of the performers discussed in this text do, Brymer terraces the dynamic levels of the sequential passages in measures 17, 19, and 21. He performs the three segments of this sequential passage at the respective volume levels of piano, mezzo piano, and mezzo forte. In accord with his practice of avoiding a declamatory style for the middle section, however, he does not increase the volume in measure 33.

In a fashion similar to his interpretation of the internal phrase grouping in the Allegro, Brymer frequently illuminates halves or sections of phrases in the Adagio that contain contrasting *tessituras*. Of particular note is his treatment of the closing portion of the phrase that commences in measure 35 (example 8.12), where he employs a quiet dynamic level. He also utilizes a timbre change beginning on the a³ above the staff. In his interpretation of the consequent half of the phrase in measures 88 to 93, Brymer performs the sequence, which also contains contrasting *tessituras,* at a quiet dynamic level, commencing with the second eighth note of bar 90. Brymer uniquely executes the consequent section of the phrase contained in bars 49 to 53 (example 8.13) at the piano level. This interpolation of a suddenly quiet volume level at the beginning of the ascending chromatic scale, coupled with a molto crescendo on the consequent portion of the phrase, results in a dramatic conclusion to the phrase, but is simultaneously less agitated than what would possibly result from executing the phrase at the printed dynamic level.

Example 8.12

Example 8.13

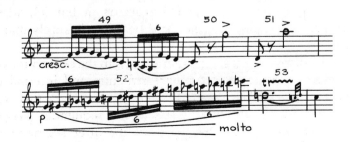

In addition to his striking utilization of dynamic phrasing in the passage in bars 49 to 53, Brymer makes notable use of both crescendos and diminuendos to enhance the harmonic progression and melodic motion of the solo line of the Adagio movement. His use of crescendos encompassing bars 5 to 7 (example 8.14) and bars 21 to 24 broadens both phrases as a result of incorporating the two shorter phrase groups included in the two passages. This treatment also provides increased impetus in the phrases as they move toward the *appoggiatura* notes on the third beats of measures 7 and 23. Brymer makes effective use of diminuendos to create a winding-down effect in the solo line in measures 92 and 93, where he decreases the volume when executing the trilled g^3 and its finish notes, and in measure 98, on the final f^2 of the Adagio. On the concluding *niente* (which in Brymer's terminology signifies a diminuendo to nothing), Brymer stresses the importance of ensemble unity between the soloist and orchestra and also expresses his belief that the orchestra must end the movement with the clarinetist.

Example 8.14

Brymer's only alteration of the articulation in the Adagio is his addition of slurs in measures 55 and 57. He slurs the quarter-note and thirty-second-note figures by the measure in those two bars.

For the cadenza of the second movement Brymer prefers either the cadenza in Mozart's Clarinet Quintet or his own original cadenza (example 8.15). In his own cadenza Brymer elongates the final g^1 and e^1 and ends the passage very quietly. He performs his own cadenza with a pause before the return of the principal Adagio theme in bar 60 (he makes no pause if he is employing the cadenza from the quintet).

Example 8.15

RONDO MOVEMENT

Brymer relates the opening phrase of the Rondo to the playing style of bowed pitches on stringed instruments. He executes the two pickup notes and the three successive eighth notes in measure 1 with lightness, as up-bowed pitches, and then performs the subsequent sixteenth notes on the fourth through sixth beats with added stress on the attacks in the manner of bowed notes.

As in his interpretation of the first two movements, Brymer makes sparing use of added expressive devices in his rendition of the Rondo. Brymer's most notable instances of expressive playing in this movement occur in the form of *tenuto* effects that he places on the eighth notes in the final three beats of measures 209, 211, and 213 and the quarter note covering the first two beats of bar 214 (example 8.16). The additional duration and weight that he allows these pitches create subtle character changes within the three segments of the sequential passage in which they appear.

Example 8.16

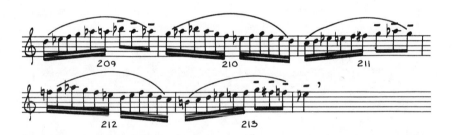

Brymer also slightly varies the posture of the trilled notes in his rendition of the Rondo. With the exception of the trill in measure 50, which he executes from the note above, Brymer begins the trills of the last movement from the written note. He does not appear to adhere to an established pattern in trill posture decisions in the Rondo; while the trilled pitch in bar 50 is preceded by a lower note in the melodic line, other trilled notes with similar melodic constructions in the solo line are executed from the written pitch.

In his interpretation of the Rondo, Brymer utilizes *rubati,* tempo fluctuations, and contrasting volume levels to elucidate the larger formal sections. He appears to call most frequently for pronounced deviation from the notated time values and established rhythmic pulse in the final movement of the concerto.

In certain instances Brymer calls attention to sectional changes in the movement through *tenuto* effects placed on pitches which precede those changes. These elongations are calculated to create illusions of changes in the established tempo of the movement. Such *tenuto* devices can be found in bar 187 (example 8.17), on the second and third eighth notes, and on the quarter note that occurs on the fourth beat of measure 207. For similar purposes Brymer endeavors to produce a surge of forward motion on the onset of the formal sections that have their beginnings in measures 57 and 137 (example 8.18). According to Brymer, Sir Thomas Beecham suggested this feeling of forward motion in the latter passage.

Example 8.17

Example 8.18

While several important American performers heighten the final return of the Rondo theme through a ritardando to a slower tempo, Brymer signals the final statement of the principal theme by means of a softer dynamic level. He prefers to execute the beginning of the final statement, which occurs in measure 334, at the pianissimo level.

In the Rondo, Brymer continues his use of dynamic contrast to highlight both the phrase construction and internal phrase groupings. He alters dynamic levels of the final movement to illuminate repeated and sequential phrases, as well as to render more apparent the related pitches within phrases and halves of phrases.

Like many other clarinetists, Brymer performs the reiterations of the phrases included in bars 84 to 87 and 226 to 230 with a contrasting

piano dynamic level. He performs the third section (bar 109) of the
sequential passage contained in measures 105 to 110 at the mezzo
forte level, rather than at the piano volume dictated in the Breitkopf
and Haertel edition. Interestingly, that section is written in the
chalumeau register, as opposed to the high *tessitura* of the first
statement of the sequence.

In his interpretation of the internal phrase structure of the Rondo
movement Brymer utilizes contrasting volumes to illuminate the
consequent sections. Passages that reflect this include measure 66
(example 8.19), which he raises in volume to mezzo forte and
performs with a deep baritone quality; bar 93 (example 8.20), which
he uniquely performs in a quiet manner, in contrast to his more
forceful approach to the *appoggiaturas* in the preceding portion of the
passage; and measure 163 (example 8.21), where he lowers the
volume to piano. (The phrase groups in measures 66 and 163 possess
contrasting *tessituras*.)

Example 8.19

Example 8.20

Example 8.21

Brymer interprets the two sixteenth-note arpeggios in measure 69
(example 8.22) as separate phrases. He does not, however, alter either
the printed dynamic level or the articulation in his execution of the
initial arpeggio and its subsequent octave transposition.

Example 8.22

Brymer also alters dynamic levels of the Rondo to compensate for intonation deficiencies of the A clarinet. He performs the passage beginning in measure 146 (example 8.23) at a pianissimo level in order to raise the pitch of the throat tones, especially e^2 and a^2, which are inherently flat. He also cautions that the orchestra must lower its dynamic level to a corresponding level in that passage in order to avoid covering the soloist.

Example 8.23

Brymer employs dynamic phrasing in the Rondo to create additional breadth in the melodic line and to provide increasing dynamic force toward the ends of consequent phrases. Passages where he crescendoes for added fullness and power include the phrase encompassing bars 47 to 51 (example 8.24), and the arpeggios in bars 88 and 89, where his crescendo extends through both measures, including the eighth-note rests, thereby combining the two measures into a single phrase.

Example 8.24

With few exceptions Brymer adheres closely to the printed articulations in his interpretation of the Rondo. In a few passages he adds slurs to the sixteenth-note runs and arpeggios, reorders articulation for phrasing purposes, or introduces tonguing on sixteenth-note runs.

Like many notable American performers, Brymer adds slurs to the sixteenth-note arpeggios in measures 20 and 21, on the first through the third beats, and in bar 84, where he slurs each of the two arpeggios. In an interesting parallel to Hasty, Brymer articulates the reiteration of the latter figure, found in measure 86, as it is indicated in the Breitkopf and Haertel edition, thereby adding variety to the articulation that he utilized in the initial statement. He slurs the scalar figure in measure 175 in two groups of six sixteenth notes (as in the two surrounding measures). Brymer also slurs the fourth and fifth eighth notes of bar 71 in a manner similar to the articulation indicated for the eighth-note passage in measure 67.

Added articulation in Brymer's version of the Rondo appears in measure 38 (example 8.25) and identically in bars 340 and 342. In each of these measures he tongues the third through sixth sixteenth notes of each half.

Brymer alters the articulation in bars 138 to 143 to create phrases that bridge inclusively from the strong first beat to the similarly emphasized fourth beat. In so doing he creates phrases that are more connected than simple measure phrases indicated in the Breitkopf and Haertel edition.

Also related to the interpretative aspects of Brymer's articulation of the Rondo is his interesting use of a breath attack for the phrase beginning in bar 35. Brymer begins the g^3 on the sixth beat of the measure with air only, without touching the tongue to the reed. The resulting effect is a gentle, quiet beginning for the phrase.

Alterations of the notation in the final movement of the concerto made by Brymer consist mainly of additions to and transpositions of the pitches indicated in the Breitkopf and Haertel edition. His added pitches consist of the commonly interpolated a^1 flat grace note before the fourth beat of bar 205 and the inclusion of the cued first violin part of the final four measures of the orchestral tutti, bars 350 to 353 (example 8.26) (his addition of the latter pitches is unique among all the interpretations studied in this text). In deference to the alleged basset clarinet version, Brymer transposes measures 311 to 313 downward an octave and substitutes f^1 notes for the c^1 pitches that occur in the passage.

Example 8.25

Example 8.26

NINE

Michele Incenzo's Interpretation

Michele Incenzo was born in Naples, Italy, where he later studied the clarinet with Giovanni Imbriani. His early years as a professional performer and teacher of his instrument were spent in Ireland. Upon his return to Italy he assumed his present position as professor of clarinet at the Rome Conservatory and works as clarinetist in several orchestras, including the Roman Festival Orchestra.

Incenzo has given his most noteworthy performances of the concerto in Ireland and in Italy. He performed the concerto on two occasions with the Radio Eireann Orchestra, under the batons of Carlo Franci and Sydney Brian. In Rome he has performed the work with the Roman Festival Orchestra under the leadership of Fritz Maraffi.

Incenzo's interpretation of the concerto is both lyrical and spirited. His approach to the solo line of the work is characterized by a flowing, *cantando* style that is frequently punctuated by accents and raised dynamic levels.

In a manner similar to Jettel and several important American clarinetists, Incenzo illuminates the character changes that occur within individual phrases. He renders many of the sixteenth-note runs and arpeggios in a *brillante* fashion and to this end avoids *tenuto* effects on the initial pitches of such rhythmic groupings. It is his belief that increased delay at the inception of *brillante* passages detracts from a desired sense of forward motion. In phrases where Incenzo wishes to heighten the brillante-espressivo contrast of

167

internal phrase groups, he frequently adds *tenuto* and *cantando* indications over eighth notes that were printed as slurred or staccato in order to reinforce the contrastingly expressive character of the pitches.

In accordance with his spirited approach to the concerto, Incenzo chooses lively tempi for the first and last movements of the work. His tempi for the Allegro and Rondo movements are not specifically attached to concrete metronomic indications, but they are very similar to the paces utilized by Hasty and Wright in their versions of the concerto.

Incenzo employs both *rubati* and fluctuations in the metric pulse in all movements of the concerto. In his approach each of these items is utilized in conjunction with the formal aspects of the work. Incenzo generally applies *rubato* when bringing forward character changes that occur within the internal parts of phrases, especially in the Rondo. The amount of *rubato* that he employs in the concerto is very similar to the frequency of *rubato* utilized in Jettel's version. Both Incenzo and Jettel appear to prefer a more romantic bent than is preferred by the other European clarinetists discussed in this book.

Incenzo frequently employs tempo fluctuations to highlight appearances of new sections in the formal structure of the concerto. His most notable deviations in tempo occur in the Adagio and the multisectioned Rondo. The propensity to actual tempo changes (even though they are subtle) is one of the more unusual features of Incenzo's interpretation of the work.

Incenzo also frequently utilizes articulation to accentuate the internal phrase groupings of the concerto. He tongues the beginnings of internal phrase groupings and carries slurs across strong pulses to a much greater degree than do most other European interpreters. Incenzo's correlation of articulation and phrasing as well as his tendency to slur more of the sixteenth-note runs and arpeggios necessitate changes in the printed articulations that are close to the four American interpretations discussed in this book.

Incenzo's choice of dynamics also reinforces his straightforward conception of the concerto. It is notable that nearly every change or addition that he makes in the indicated dynamic markings of the Breitkopf and Haertel edition results in increased volume levels.

With the exception of changes regarding residual printer's errors in the Breitkopf and Haertel edition, Incenzo makes no notational changes. He transposes two passages in the Allegro movement an octave higher in deference to the alleged original version of the concerto.

ALLEGRO MOVEMENT

Incenzo's conception of the solo line of the concerto is much akin to the approach that might be taken by a singer. In an attempt to maintain a lyrical style for the movement, Incenzo avoids a *secco* staccato and in a number of passages adds *tenuto* effects and slurs over pitches. Like many other clarinetists, he believes that the excessive separation of pitches caused by short staccato tonguing detracts from a smooth flow of the melodic line.

The addition of *tenuto* styles for increased breadth in the line is especially notable in three passages of the Allegro. In bar 113 (example 9.1) he replaces the legato indication of the Breitkopf and Haertel edition with *tenuto* markings (interestingly, several of the other clarinetists analyzed in this text utilize a poco ritardando in this passage). In measure 152 (example 9.2) Incenzo adds *tenuto* markings over the triplets on the first three beats; he also adds a *cantando* indication, which creates a contrast in mood with the brillante sixteenth notes in the two preceding measures. Finally, in measure 224 (example 9.3) he performs the eighth notes on the third and fourth beats with *tenuto* effects rather than the indicated staccato.

Example 9.1

Example 9.2

Example 9.3

Passages in which he couples slurs with a legato indication for a more *cantabile* effect include measures 108 to 115 (see example 9.1) and 152 to 154 (example 9.2), the sixteenth-note arpeggios in measures 73 and 83, the scalar runs in bar 142, the sixteenth-note runs in measure 314, the dotted quarter- and eighth-note figure in bar 315, and each of the sixteenth-note arpeggios in measures 326 and 327. While several of the clarinetists discussed in this book slur all of the sixteenth notes in bars 108 and 109, Incenzo is the only artist who connects the sixteenth-note runs and arpeggios contained in bars 110 and 111 within a single slur (example 9.4).

Example 9.4

In contrast to the *cantabile* aspects of his rendition of the first movement, Incenzo interjects forceful articulation for increased emphasis of specific pitches in a number of passages. In several of the agitato passages he utilizes either accents or staccato for increased vigor and expressiveness. He accents the syncopated notes in measures 188 and 189 (example 9.5) and the pitches that conclude the phrase in bars 191 and 192. He also accents the syncopated notes and the concluding half notes of bars 213 and 214 (example 9.6). This phrase provides a dramatic conclusion to the solo portion of the agitato passage that ends the development section of the Allegro movement. Incenzo is the only clarinetist discussed in this text who includes these accents and also accents the first quarter note of measure 224 (example 9.3), which is a continuation of the accented pitches in the previous measure.

Example 9.5

Example 9.6

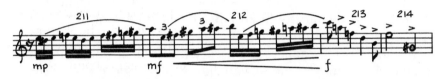

It is of note that Incenzo is also the only major interpreter of the concerto whose version requires increased punctuation for the eighth notes on the third and fourth beats of bar 189 (example 9.5) and the fifth and sixth eighth triplets in bar 293 (example 9.7). In both passages he executes the later pitches in a staccato fashion as a continuation of the forceful punctuation that he introduces in the earlier portions of the phrases.

Example 9.7

In additon to use of *rubato* in passages in which it is used by most other performers, such as in bar 126, on the sixteenth notes preceding a strong cadence, and on the quasi cadenza contained in bars 198 and 199, Incenzo introduces a unique fluctuation in the established rhythmic values in measures 311 and 312 (example 9.8). In these two measures he performs the triplets on the third and fourth beats slightly slower than tempo and then regains the tempo on the first beat of the succeeding bars.

Example 9.8

Incenzo's approach to the trills of the first movement is similar to the approaches observed in American renditions of the concerto. Incenzo utilizes both inverted and noninverted trills and appears not to follow any particular rule in his selection of either posture. Incenzo initiates the trills in bars 74, 268, and 342 from above the written pitch and plays the remaining trills of the Allegro from the written note. Like a number of other artists, he adds finish notes to the trilled half notes in measure 225 (example 9.3).

Incenzo does not adhere to a predetermined metronome marking for the Allegro movement. As with the other two movements, Incenzo prefers a tempo of the moment. His usual tempo for the Allegro, however, is close to 120 quarter notes per minute.

Incenzo utilizes both dynamic contrast and tempo deviation to make the overall formal structure more apparent to the listener. As is the case in most interpretations, Incenzo prefers a poco ritardando in the orchestral accompaniment in measure 250. In addition to that change, he introduces a slight reduction in the tempo in measure 248 (example 9.9) on the last four pitches of the sixteenth-note run.

Example 9.9

Incenzo utilizes volume differences to accentuate both the phrase structure and the interiors of individual phrases. He prefers to illuminate repeated phrases, such as those in bars 180 and 182, through the use of an echo effect on the reiterated material (forte and then pianissimo). His treatment of sequential phrases is unique to his interpretation. Incenzo utilizes an interesting reverse terraced effect in the sequential phrase group encompassing bars 108 to 111 (example 9.4). He begins both the first and the second segments forte and couples them with diminuendos, and initiates the third segment mezzo forte and follows it with a crescendo to the conclusion of the passage. Incenzo also interprets the sequential passage in measures 296 to 300 (example 9.10) in a unique fashion. He negotiates the first two sections of the phrase group piano, coupled with a crescendo and diminuendo within the measure, and begins the third group at an identical volume level but crescendoes through the succeeding measures to the end of the phrase.

Example 9.10

Another notable feature of Incenzo's interpretation of the phrase structure of the Allegro is his employment of increased volume levels at the middles of phrases for purposes of expansion and additional lyricism. Characteristic examples of such increased volume levels appear in bars 69 to 71 (example 9.11), where he carries the initial forte dynamic level of the phrase through the c^3 in bar 71, and in measures 206 to 210 (example 9.12), where he deletes the piano markings on the higher *tessitura* material in bars 207 and 209.

Example 9.11

Example 9.12

In addition to his frequent use of dynamics for phrasing, Incenzo relies heavily on added slurs to delineate groups of related pitches in the phrase structure of the Allegro movement. Like a number of American performers, Incenzo often adds slurs to carry phrases across bar lines or to bridge the strong pulse of the third beat of certain measures.

Incenzo's addition of slurs to outline phrase groups is unique in a number of passages of the first movement. Such passages include measures 71 and 72 (example 9.11), where he connects the second through fifth eighth notes in one group and then the sixth through eighth notes and the dotted half note of the succeeding bar; measures 85 to 90, in which he adds slurs to create three expansive sections, two of which span three bars; measures 117 to 119 (example 9.13), and identically 121 to 123, where he adds a slur across two successive bar lines; bar 124 (example 9.14), and identically bar 312, in which he connects the dotted quarter note and eighth note with the f³ sharp eighth-note triplet on the third beat; bar 130 (example 9.15), where he connects the dotted quarter note on the second half of the measure with the eighth- and sixteenth-note figure on the first part of the succeeding measure; and bars 174 and 175 (example 9.16), and also 177 to 180, where he slurs across bar lines to create expansive phrase groups.

Example 9.13

Example 9.14

Example 9.15

Example 9.16

In addition to passages where Incenzo interjects staccato for increased vigor, he also calls for added staccato for purposes of uniformity and variety within the solo line of the Allegro. Interestingly, Incenzo tongues the eighth notes on the second beat of bar 130 (example 9.15), and also in bars 317 and 318. This alteration of the printed Breitkopf and Haertel edition results in a matching of articulation of the closing theme with the tonguing indicated for the principal theme. Like Gigliotti, Incenzo also tongues the fourth sixteenth note of every beat in measures 143 and 144 (example 9.17), and in measures 331 to 333, as a variation from the articulation patterns in the preceding passages.

Example 9.17

Incenzo alters the printed notation as well for the sake of uniformity in his performance. He changes the second and third sixteenth notes of measure 97 (example 9.18) to d^1 and e^1 pitches to match the intervallic sequence of the passage with the notational pattern that appears in bar 285 of the recapitulation.

Example 9.18

Incenzo's other notational changes for the Allegro take the form of octave transpositions. He raises the printed pitches in the second halves of both bars 146 and 147, as well as the sixteenth notes on the first and second beats of measure 330.

ADAGIO MOVEMENT

In his performance of the Adagio, Incenzo utilizes ornamentation and *rubato* to augment the lyrical effect that he has established in the initial movement of the concerto. In many of his embellishments of the solo line, as well as his fluctuations in notated rhythms, his rendition is entirely unique.

Incenzo's approach to both the indicated grace notes and turns of the movement differs sharply from the approaches of other performers. Incenzo executes the grace notes in measures 7, 23, and 86 before the beat and avoids giving excessive duration to the pitches. Also in a unique manner, he negotiates the first three turn notes in beats one and two of measure 39 (example 9.19) within the first half of each respective beat, thus allowing a long time value for the fourth turn note. In making this alteration, it is his intention to accentuate the stepwise linear progression in each of the two figures. The resulting rhythm of each of the two affected beats closely resembles four thirty-second notes which are followed by sixteenth notes on the respective upbeats.

Example 9.19

While Incenzo does not utilize an inordinate amount of *rubato* in his interpretation of the Adagio, his use of rhythmic elasticity in several passages of the movement is noteworthy. In measure 55 (example 9.20) Incenzo calls for poco *rubato* on the first and second beats, followed by a *rallentando* in the third beat, a style which he repeats in bar 57. In a manner unique to his rendition of the second movement, Incenzo continues a broadening of the time values of the final pitches of bars 52 (example 9.21) and 94 (example 9.22) into the respective succeeding measures.

Example 9.20

Example 9.21

Example 9.22

As he does in the first movement, Incenzo utilizes a change in tempo to signal the beginning of a new section of the formal structure in the Adagio. It is noteworthy that Incenzo is the only clarinetist discussed in this text who performs the final codetta, beginning in measure 93 (example 9.22) and continuing to the end of the movement, at a slightly slower tempo. He also raises the volume level of that section to mezzo forte.

Interestingly, Incenzo does not change the tempo of the middle section of the movement. He does, however, alter his mental conception of the meter from a feeling of three beats per measure (in quarter notes) in the A section of the Adagio to six beats per bar (in eighth notes) in the B section. Like all of the other artists discussed in this book, Incenzo performs the return of the A section at a quieter dynamic level than that of the initial statement.

Incenzo also parallels other clarinetists in his use of dynamics to illuminate the internal phrase structure of the Adagio. He utilizes contrasting volume levels to mark reiterated phrases and employs terraced dynamics in conjunction with the sequential passages contained in the second movement. Of special note is the increase in volume that Incenzo utilizes at the phrase beginning in measure 83 (example 9.23). He raises the dynamic level of this phrase, which is coincidentally the initial passage of the coda, from piano to forte and then performs the repeated phrase in bar 85 as an echo, at the pianissimo level.

Example 9.23

Incenzo relies heavily on articulation to set apart the internal phrase groupings of the Adagio movement. As he does in the Allegro, Incenzo frequently slurs groups of related pitches, both within measures, for example in bars 2 and 4 and all subsequent appearances of that theme, and across bar lines. Slurred phrase groups that are unique to his interpretation occur in bar 74 (example 9.24), where the sixteenth notes on the first beat are slurred to the quarter note on the second beat; bars 90 and 91 (example 9.25), in which Incenzo bridges all of the eighth notes in measure 90 and the first sixtuplet note of bar 91 under a single slur; and measures 93 to 95 (example 9.22), where Incenzo slurs across the bar lines from the third beats of bars 93 and 94 to the pitches on the first beats of the respective succeeding measures.

Example 9.24

Example 9.25

For the cadenza of the Adagio, Incenzo performs his own original material (example 9.26). Obviously, Incenzo's cadenza therefore deviates greatly from the cadenzas of other clarinetists. It should be noted, however, that the basic linear construction of his cadenza resembles the melodic framework of the cadenza in the Ricordi edition of the concerto.

Example 9.26

RONDO MOVEMENT

Like all of the other clarinetists discussed in this book, Incenzo views the Rondo movement as the liveliest of the three. His view is reflected in his rendition through frequent use of accents and his avoidance of *tenuto* playing at the beginnings of runs and arpeggios.

In his performance of the solo line of the final movement, Incenzo adds a number of original accents in addition to those appearing in the Breitkopf and Haertel edition. For additional punctuation in his delivery of the solo line, Incenzo adds accents to the dotted quarter notes in measures 2 (example 9.27) and 6 (example 9.28) and in all similar appearances of the Rondo theme. In like manner he accents the dotted quarter notes that appear in bars 39 (example 9.29), 72, and 224 (with the exception of the dotted quarter in bar 224, which appears on the fourth beat, all accented dotted quarters appear on the first beats of the respective measures). Incenzo also adds accents to the successive dotted quarter notes in bars 151 to 153. Interestingly, he carries the series of accented dotted quarter notes in bars 161 and 162 farther by accenting the dotted quarter note that is tied to an eighth note in bar 163 (example 9.30); this playing style is repeated in measures 165 to 167. He also accents the dotted half note in bars 181 and 325.

Example 9.27

Example 9.28

Example 9.29

Example 9.30

As he does in the previous movements, Incenzo varies the posture of the trills in the Rondo movement. He performs the trills in measures 50, 177, 321, and 296 in an inverted manner; he negotiates the remaining trills, in measures 315, 317, and 345, from the written pitch.

Incenzo's interpretation of the solo line of the Rondo is further characterized by his illumination of the contrasting phrase groupings. He differentiates between the expressive and brillante qualities of pitch groups within the phrase contained in measures 35 to 38 (example 9.31). He performs the eighth notes in the first half of the phrase espressivo and the final sixteenth-note run in a brillante fashion. He varies the attitude of the passage in measures 88 to 97 (example 9.32) in a reverse manner. Incenzo contrasts the brillante sixteenth-note arpeggios in the initial portion of the phrase with the espressivo eighth notes in bar 94. He further marks the contrasting character of the eighth-note section by performing measures 93 and 94 at a slightly slower tempo than the surrounding bars. He also creates a unique brillante-espressivo contrast in phrase groups through his utilization of a *più mosso* style in bars 208 to 217 (example

9.33), and a dramatically slower tempo with the eighth note as the pulse in measures 220 and 221.

Example 9.31

Example 9.32

Example 9.33

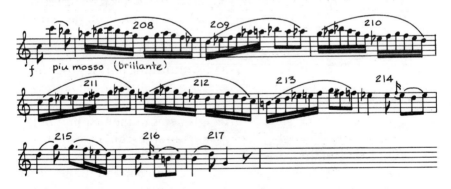

In addition to his utilization of tempo changes to mark character differences within phrases, Incenzo alters the speed of the meter to delineate the larger formal sections of the final movement. Tempo changes that mark new sections of the formal structure of the Rondo include a poco *più mosso* tempo at bar 301 (example 9.34), which begins the coda, and the *meno mosso* speed from measure 334 to the end of the movement. While the first of the two tempo changes is unique to Incenzo's interpretation, the second is utilized by a number of both American and European clarinetists.

Example 9.34

Incenzo also highlights the appearance of several of the larger sections of the formal structure of the Rondo movement through increased volume levels. He raises the volume level from piano to mezzo forte in bars 35 (example 9.31) and 137 (example 9.35), and adds a forte indication for the section beginning in measure 187 (example 9.36).

Example 9.35

Example 9.36

Incenzo does not outline the repeated and sequential phrases of the Rondo through dynamic change as he does those of the first two movements. He does, however, accentuate the phrase sections that exhibit contrasting *tessituras* and to this end adds forte markings to the masculine phrase halves that appear in measures 173 (example 9.37) and 183.

Example 9.37

Incenzo's interpretation of the phrasing of the Rondo also incorporates the use of articulation. In the final movement he frequently adds slurs to mark segments of phrases that extend across bar lines.

Of special note are the series of phrase groups in the Rondo that result from Incenzo's reordered articulations. His changes in the printed articulations of bars 137 to 144 (example 9.35) create five short groups of related pitches, each beginning on the sixth beat of a measure, as in the initial segment of the series. Incenzo orders the articulation of the phrase groups contained in measures 146 to 157 and 222 to 224 in a similar fashion. Both of these phrase segments and those he reworks in bars 332 to 334 are unique to his version of the final movement.

Other articulation changes in the Rondo made by Incenzo consist of slurs for increased facility and brilliance on sixteenth-note runs and arpeggios and alterations for purposes of uniformity. As in the previous movements, in the Rondo Incenzo frequently deviates from the articulations printed in the Breitkopf and Haertel edition. Although his alterations in articulation vary from those made by his European counterparts, he does not make any changes in the tongued and slurred notes that do not already appear in the American interpretations that have been described in this text.

Incenzo's notational changes in the Rondo include corrections of the residual printer's errors, such as in bar 169, where he replaces the a^1 with a b^1 flat, and the addition of the a^1 flat grace note before the g^1 in measure 205. Incenzo is one of the few European clarinetists who perform measure 205 of the Rondo with the additional embellishment.

TEN

Summary and Conclusions

The review of eight important contemporary interpretations of the Mozart Clarinet Concerto reveals not only a striking number of similarities, but interesting differences, in the musical thinking and performance techniques of eight notable clarinetists. Important differences in the renditions of the work by Hasty, Marcellus, Gigliotti, Wright, Jettel, Delécluse, Brymer, and Incenzo can be observed in their treatments of the melodic line, ornamentation, tempi, *rubato,* articulation, dynamics, approach to formal aspects, attention to the harmonic background, and changes in notation.

While each of the clarinetists places great emphasis on expressive performance of the melodic line, Hasty and Gigliotti appear to utilize a more consciously structured approach to their introduction of expressive devices. This is especially true of Hasty, who employs *tenuto* effects or legato tonguing for the expressive rendition of all *appoggiatura* figures and successive ascending major and minor thirds in the Allegro movement. Wright and Jettel frequently utilize *tenuto* playing and legato tonguing to enhance the expressiveness of the melodic line, but in a less structured manner. Marcellus uses *tenuto* stylisms to accentuate Mozart's unique compositional trait of juxtaposing brillante florid passages with sustained espressivo phrases.

Another element of contrast in the melodic line, the opposition of high and low *tessitura* phrases, is highlighted through dynamic change by all of the clarinetists cited. In addition to performing the low range phrases loudly and the contrasting high range phrases softly, Wright and especially Brymer incorporate changes in tonal color as well (very full and broad for the low notes and thin and small for the high pitches). The resulting contrast of the opposing phrases, not unlike opposing male and female roles, creates an operatic color in those two versions of the concerto.

Accents are employed by each of the clarinetists to punctuate or emphasize single pitches in the line and to reinforce declamatory passages, especially those which conclude large sections in the formal structure of the Allegro and Rondo movements. Incenzo makes the most frequent use of accents in his approach to the concerto. The resulting effects render his performance perhaps the most dramatic of the interpretations studied in this book.

In approaching trills in the work and the grace notes in the Adagio movement, Hasty, Marcellus, Brymer, and Incenzo give priority to the musical effect of the devices in choosing the manner of execution, rather than adhering to the commonly accepted rules of performance practice followed by Gigliotti and Wright, who execute most trills in the inverted position. Jettel and Delécluse negotiate all trills from the written pitch; Hasty, Marcellus, and Incenzo perform most of the trills in an inverted fashion. It is noteworthy that Hasty, Marcellus, and Incenzo perform the grace notes in the Adagio with shorter durations than the sixteenth-note length allotted to them by the other five performers.

Each of the eight performers favors lively tempi for the first and last movements of the concerto. Hasty, Wright, Jettel, Delécluse, and Incenzo prefer the fastest tempi (♩ = 120 for the Allegro and ♩. = 84 to 88 for the Rondo). Delécluse indicates the quickest tempo range for the Allegro (♩ = 120 to 126). Brymer's choice of tempo for the Allegro (♩ = 116) is slightly more leisurely than the remaining performers.

All of the clarinetists except Delécluse include deviations in the rhythmic pulse in all three movements of the concerto in addition to the two fermatas indicated in the Breitkopf and Haertel edition of the Allegro movement; Delécluse makes additional alterations in the rhythmic pulse of the Adagio movement only. Almost all interpolated tempo deviations utilized by the performers are in conjunction with beginnings or closings of larger formal sections within the three movements. In addition to *rubato* on small groups of pitches, Hasty and Jettel also use tempo deviations in passages that involve adjacent phrases from two to four measures in length. Interestingly, Hasty and Delécluse are the only clarinetists of the eight who do not broaden the tempo of the final return of the principal theme of the Rondo movement.

Articulation is utilized by Hasty, Marcellus, Gigliotti, and Incenzo to emphasize particular pitches within the solo line, to increase variety, and to delineate the phrase structure of the work. Conversely, the renditions of Wright, Jettel, Delécluse, and Brymer are characterized by a much stricter adherence to the articulations printed in the Breitkopf and Haertel edition. The approach taken by these performers results in more frequent articulation and less dependence on the device for musical effects than is the case with the other renditions.

In addition to the established uses for articulation, Hasty employs the device for the emphasis of changes of direction in the melodic line and for the maintenance of symmetry in odd-numbered successions of sixteenth notes in the Rondo. Wright frequently utilizes articulation for interpretive aspects in his rendition of the concerto, but he does not utilize articulation in conjunction with phrasing. He tongues the last notes of phrases that extend across bar lines instead of slurring them as other performers frequently do.

Regarding the length of tongued sixteenth notes in the Allegro and Rondo movements, each of the performers varies the duration of short articulated notes in accordance with the expressive quality desired. Among the artists discussed in this book, Marcellus and Incenzo prefer the longest average length of tongued notes, and Wright and Delécluse prefer the shortest. It is also of note that, unlike other clarinetists, Wright does not perform the tongued sixteenth notes in the Rondo with shorter staccato than the articulated sixteenth notes of the Allegro.

In each of the performances, the clarinetist's choices of dynamic levels and his utilization of dynamic phrasing are closely associated both with the overall formal structure of the concerto and with its smaller details. Especially in the interpretations of Hasty, Marcellus, and Incenzo the return of large segments in the architecture of the work is often signaled by changes in volume. Changes in dynamic levels are frequently utilized to highlight short reiterations of phrases. Perhaps the greatest number of dynamic changes, in the form of quasi echoes in conjunction with repeated phrases and volume changes for other musical effects such as contrasting *tessituras,* are made by Gigliotti, Delécluse, and Brymer. Hasty combines volume changes with articulation alterations to accentuate short repeated phrases. Brymer's use of contrasting tonal focus in conjunction with high and low *tessitura* passages is one of the unique features of his interpretation. Conversely, Wright avoids volume changes on repeated phrases; he prefers to stress repetitions through changes in tonal color and in articulation.

A noteworthy contrast in dynamic levels throughout the concerto exists in the volume levels most frequently chosen by Delécluse and Incenzo. While Delécluse tends to dynamic levels predominantly quieter than those printed in the edition, Incenzo very frequently raises the indicated volume levels.

One of the outstanding features of Marcellus's interpretation of the concerto is his attempt to create a broad, expansive phrase structure. In his approach, sequential dynamic phrasing is employed to draw together short groups of pitches and thereby to form more lengthy phrases. While Gigliotti does not ignore the overall structure of the work, it would appear that, of all the players discussed in this text, he is the most concerned with small, internal groupings of pitches. This is especially true of phrases that extend across bar lines and groups of pitches that are carried to strong internal beats. An interesting exception to the clarinetists' various renditions of large formal segments in a manner identical to interpretations of the original appearances is Wright's performance of the Rondo. In this case, the principal theme of the movement is varied with each reappearance.

In terms of the harmonic elements of the work, the nonharmonic tones in the solo line are the most frequently recognized and highlighted by all of the performers. While each of the players demonstrates awareness of the harmonic scheme of the concerto, including the more conspicuous altered chords, Hasty places the greatest emphasis on these features in his interpretation. In a number of passages he accentuates the chord member contained in the solo line through articulations or dynamic phrasing.

Each performer's approach to the instrument is highly varied and complex. The most significant variations of approach to the clarinet, which in turn have bearing on the rendition of the concerto, are seen in the philosophies of articulation and finger motion expounded by Gigliotti.

Gigliotti's articulation and finger motion represent the lightest motion of tongue and fingers utilized by the eight performers. He believes that the clarinetist must avoid a heavy motion of the tongue as it breaks the air column. The fingers are moved lightly toward the tone holes of the instrument to avoid an extraneous accented beginning of slurred pitches. Conversely, the short style of articulation preferred by Wright for the Allegro and Rondo movements, which he calls "ball bouncing," results in a quite different mode of performance of the work.

Interestingly, the mechanical considerations of the performances, such as the fingering systems and mouthpiece-reed combinations utilized by the clarinetists, have surprisingly little effect on the ultimate interpretations of the concerto. With the exception of Jettel, each of the artist-teachers perform on a French model Boehm system clarinet with a French oriented mouthpiece-reed combination. Jettel's instrument is a German model that combines the Oehler fingering system and a German mouthpiece-reed combination.

While each of the eight clarinetists includes a multitude of carefully conceived small events in his performance of the work, none seems to lose sight of the overall structure. The greatest number of interpretative devices included in individual measures of the concerto are found in Hasty's rendition. However, he also expresses an almost equal interest in the details of the larger structure of the work. Perhaps the smallest number of single events, with the exception of character changes within phrases, are found in the interpretations of Marcellus, Wright, and Brymer. Therefore, one can assume that these three performers have the greatest interest in the broader aspects of the formal structure of the concerto.

The frequency and method of usage of each of the devices and approaches delineated above determines the degree of romantic or classical bias of the performer. All of the interpretations studied in this text appear to be oriented toward a romantic stylistic approach. This bias is best evidenced with regard to several features of performance—espressivo devices, ornamentation, and deviations in tempo, including quasi cadenzas, ritardandos, and broadened tempi. Perhaps Delécluse's version, with its minimal use of *rubato,* most closely follows the traditions of classical interpretation.

Notes

[1]Otto E. Deutsch, *Mozart's Catalogue of His Works, 1756–1791,* facsimile (New York: Herbert Reichmer, n.d.), p. 36.

[2]Ernst Hess, "Anton Stadler," *Die Musik in Geschichte und Gegenwart,* ed. Friedrich Blume, 14 vols. (Kassel und Basel: Berenreiter, 1949–51), 12: col. 1119.

[3]Emily Anderson, *Letters of Mozart and His Family,* 3 vols. (London: Macmillan and Co., 1938), 3:1437.

[4]Friedrich Blume, "The Concertos: (I) Their Sources," *The Mozart Companion,* ed. Howard Candler and Landon Robbins (New York: W. W. Norton & Co., 1956), p. 207.

[5]Jean Massin and Brigette Massin, *Wolfgang Amadeus Mozart,* 2 vols. (Paris: Librairie Artheme Fayard, 1970), 1:1160.

[6]Anderson, *Letters of Mozart and His Family,* 3:1479.

[7]Ludwig Köchel, *Chronologish-thematisches Verzeichnis sämtlicher Tonwerke W. A. Mozart,* 6th ed., rev. Alfred Einstein (Leipzig: Breitkopf and Haertel, 1964), p. 723.

[8]Anderson, *Letters of Mozart and His Family,* 3:1455.

[9]Köchel, *Verzeichnis,* p. 723.

[10]Louis Biancolli, *The Mozart Handbook* (Cleveland: World Publishing Co., 1954), p. 384.

[11]Otto Jahn, *The Life of Mozart,* 4th ed., trans. Pauling Townsend, 3 vols. (New York: Edwin F. Kalmus, 1905–1907), 1:398.

[12]Blume, "The Concertos," p. 208.

[13]Jahn, *The Life of Mozart,* 1:398.

[14]Quoted in Blume, "The Concertos," p. 208.

[15]Paul Nettl, *Mozart and Masonry* (New York: Da Capo Press, 1970), p. 121.

[16]Jahn, *The Life of Mozart,* 2:72.

[17]Anderson, *Letters of Mozart and His Family,* 2:948.

[18]Pamela Weston, *Clarinet Virtuosi of the Past* (London: Robert Hale, 1971), p. 47.

[19]Adam Carse, *The Orchestra in the Eighteenth Century* (Cambridge: W. Heffer and Sons, 1940), p. 179.

[20]Ibid., p. 36.

[21]F. Geoffrey Rendall, *The Clarinet,* 2d ed. rev. (London: Ernest Benn, 1957), p. 83.

[22]Carse, *The Orchestra in the Eighteenth Century,* p. 36.

[23]Biancolli, *The Mozart Handbook,* p. 330.

[24]Jahn, *The Life of Mozart,* 2:465.

[25]Otto Deutsch, *Mozart: A Documentary Biography* (Palo Alto: Stanford University Press, 1965), p. 327.

[26]Alfred Einstein, *Mozart: His Character and His Work* (New York: Oxford University Press, 1945), pp. 194–195.

[27]Hess, "Anton Stadler," 12: col. 1119.

[28]George Dazeley, "The Original Text of Mozart's Clarinet Concerto," *Music Review,* 9 (1948): 166–72.

[29]Quoted in Weston, *Clarinet Virtuosi of the Past,* pp. 48–49.

[30]Ibid., pp. 47–48.

[31]Deutsch, *Mozart: A Documentary Biography,* p. 327.

[32]Hess, "Anton Stadler," 12: col. 1119.

[33]Jahn, *The Life of Mozart,* p. 309.

[34]Hess, "Anton Stadler," 12: col. 1119.

[35]Quoted in Weston, *Clarinet Virtuosi of the Past,* pp. 48–49.

[36]Deutsch, *Mozart: A Documentary Biography,* p. 585.

[37]Hess, "Anton Stadler," 12: col. 1119.

[38]Ibid.

[39]Ernst Hess, "Die ursprüngliche Gestalt des Klarinett-Konzertes, K.V. 622," *Mozart-Jarbuch* (1967); p. 21.

[40]Rendall, *The Clarinet,* p. 83.

[41]Dazeley, "The Original Text of Mozart's Clarinet Concerto," pp. 166–72; Kratochvil, "Ist die heute gebrauchliche Fassung des Klarinettenkonzerts und des Klarinettenquintetts von Mozart authentisch?," *Beitrage zur Musikwissenschaft* (1960); 27–34; Hess, "Die ursprüngliche Gestalt," pp. 18–30.

[42]Dazeley, "The Original Text of Mozart's Clarinet Concerto," p. 166.

[43]Weston, *Clarinet Virtuosi of the Past,* pp. 46–58.

[44]Cited in Hess, "Die ursprüngliche Gestalt," pp. 18–30.

[45]Kratochvil, "Ist die heute gebrauchliche Fassung des Klarinettenkonzerts . . ."

[46]Dazeley, "The Original Text of Mozart's Clarinet Concerto," pp. 166–72.

[47]Ibid.

[48]Roland Tenshert, "Fragment eines Klarinetten-Quintetts von W. A. Mozart," *Zeitschrift fur Musikwissenschaft* 13 (1930–31):218.

[49]Hess, "Die ursprüngliche Gestalt," pp. 18–30.

[50]Weston, *Clarinet Virtuosi of the Past,* p. 48.

[51]Quoted in Hess, "Die ursprüngliche Gestalt," pp. 18–30.

[52]Ibid.

[53]Ibid.

[54]Dazeley, "The Original Text of Mozart's Clarinet Concerto," pp. 166–72.

[55]Hermann Abert, *W. A. Mozart* (Leipzig: Breitkopf and Haertel, 1955), 1:599.

[56]Ibid.

[57]Ibid.

[58]Ibid.

[59]Adam Carse, *The History of Orchestration* (New York: E. P. Dutton and Co., 1925), p. 190.

[60]Rudolf Gerber, *Eulenberg Miniature Score, Mozart Clarinet Concerto, K. 622* (London: Ernest Eulenberg, 1937), foreword.

[61]Biancolli, *The Mozart Handbook,* p. 386.